Wonderful Exchange

Wonderful Exchange

An Exploration of Silent Prayer

Alexander Ryrie

Paulist Press
New York/Mahwah, N.J.

Scripture quotations are taken from the Revised Standard Version Bible © 1971 and 1952 and the New Revised Standard Version Bible © 1989 The National Council of the Churches of Christ in the USA

Cover design by Diego Linares
Book design by Lynn Else

This edition published by arrangement with the Canterbury Press Norwich (a publishing imprint of Hymns Ancient & Modern Limited, a registered charity).

Library of Congress Cataloging-in-Publication Data

Ryrie, Alexander.
    Wonderful exchange : an exploration of silent prayer / Alexander Ryrie.
        p.   cm.
    Includes bibliographical references (p.   ).
    ISBN 0-8091-4325-9 (alk. paper)
    1. Prayer—Christianity. 2. Silence—Religious aspects—Christianity.
3. Contemplation. I. Title.

BV215.R97 2005
248.3′2—dc22

                                                    2004030504

Published in 2005 by
Paulist Press
997 Macarthur Boulevard
Mahwah, New Jersey, 07430

www.paulistpress.com

Printed and bound in the
United States of America

Contents

The Lord is in his holy temple;
let all the earth keep silence before him.

Habakkuk 2:20

In Christ your Son
our life and yours are brought together
in a wonderful exchange.

Scottish Liturgy 1982

Foreword

Wisdom is to discern the true rhythm of things:
joy is to move, to dance to that rhythm.

Too much can be made of the distinctions between the different expressions of Christian spirituality. They all derive from the experience of what God has done and is doing in us and among us. While emphases differ, their validity is their congruence with the good news of Jesus Christ in the scriptures. As the various instruments in an orchestra make their special contribution to the symphony, so we delight in the extra dimension that each tradition brings to the living out of the Christian faith.

The present wide interest in spirituality seems to indicate that, in the midst of all the current uncertainties that we meet in contemporary life, despite its relative comfort and technological advance, there is felt a need to reconnect with our spiritual roots and find a deeper purpose for living.

It is an exploration into the way that spiritual practice can affect our lifestyle, work, relationships, our view of creation, patterns of prayer and worship, and responsibilities in the wider world.

Many books, of course, have been written in all of these areas, and in each tradition classic commentaries are available that can never be surpassed. The aim here is to meet the needs of those searching for or beginning to explore the journey inward into their inmost being and outward to relationship with people and the whole of creation.

This book is a description of the process and experience of silent prayer, a way of praying that helps us to be more in touch with our inner selves and God within.

Bishop Graham Chadwick
Salisbury

Preface

This book is written in the hope that it will be of help to
some people in their praying. It is in some ways a sequel to
my earlier book, *Silent Waiting: The Biblical Roots of
Contemplative Spirituality;* but here I attempt to discuss the
subject of silent prayer from a different perspective and in a
more general way. In addition to expressing other thoughts,
I also develop more fully some of the topics discussed in the
earlier book.

In my reflections on this subject I have been influenced
by the works of many spiritual writers, but I have also been
helped by a considerable number of people who have spoken
freely with me about their inner life of prayer, and from
whom I have learned and gained a great deal. This has been
especially valuable, since my intention is to write about
prayer in a way that fits in with the experience of ordinary
people. I make no attempt to discuss the higher levels of contemplative prayer or to describe its lofty peaks; I aim rather
to explore what silent prayer can mean for those of us who
do not get beyond the foothills.

In writing the book I have tried to use inclusive language
as far as possible, but I have found no sensible, readily
usable, and theologically appropriate alternative to a gen-
dered pronoun for God. My usage does not mean, however,
that I am unaware of issues of gender. I also hope that the

inevitably noninclusive language of earlier writers whom I quote will not prevent modern readers from listening to the truths they express.

In my discussion of the "passions" in chapters 3 and 4, I have repeated some thoughts and reused some paragraphs from an article entitled "Prayer and the Struggle against Evil" which appeared in *Fairacres Chronicle* 36, no. 1 (Spring 2003). I am grateful to the SLG Press for allowing me to do this. Quotations from the Bible are taken from the Revised Standard Version or the New Revised Standard Version.

I owe a debt of gratitude to Hilary Ogilvie for reading the chapters as they have been written and for drawing attention to necessary corrections and advisable improvements; and especially to my wife, Isabel, not only for her constant encouragement but also for reading the text and making valuable suggestions.

Since in the matter of prayer we are all beginners and learners, I shall be glad to hear and learn from the comments that any readers may care to make.

Alexander Ryrie
Melrose, Scotland

Introduction

This book offers a description of one approach to silent prayer. This kind of prayer is often referred to as "contemplation" or sometimes "meditation." But these words carry a lot of baggage from the past; to some they may suggest that praying in this way is something extraordinary and special, undertaken by a few specialists, reserved mainly for holy men and women of prayer. I believe that praying in this way is not only for the specialist but is something that can be done by any committed person; and so I prefer to avoid the traditional terms and use instead the simple phrase, the "prayer of silence."

A "wonderful exchange" is a way of describing the kind of relationship we have with God in the prayer of silence. The phrase is found in some Roman Catholic and Anglican liturgies, but it reflects a theological understanding found most of all in the Eastern Orthodox Church. It usually refers to God's coming among us in Jesus Christ, but it can be extended to provide a helpful way of thinking about silent prayer. God not only came to us in Jesus Christ; he also comes to us personally, and in the prayer of silence we engage in what I will call a reciprocal or mutual relationship with him. Prayer of this kind is a two-sided enterprise, in which we are open to God and he to us; there is a give-and-take, a to-ing and fro-ing between us and God, a kind of shared activity. To see prayer in this way is to add a special dimension to it. My intention in this book is to explore this wonderful exchange and its meaning for our prayer.

Like many others in recent times, I have found myself especially drawn to the spiritual writers of the Orthodox tradition of the Christian East, including Syriac writers. A great deal has been written about this way of prayer by people of other Christian traditions. We can learn about it from the writings of John of the Cross, Julian of Norwich, Thomas Merton, and a great many others who have explored the prayer of silence in depth. But I believe that the Orthodox tradition offers insights into a way of silent prayer that can be especially meaningful today, even for those of us who do not belong to that tradition. The account of silent prayer that I present here draws very heavily on Orthodox thought. I refer throughout the book to Orthodox writings, both ancient and recent; and at the end of each chapter I have gathered together a few short quotations from Orthodox writers that illustrate some of the points being made in that chapter. The book is not an exposition of Orthodox spirituality, and it does not claim to represent an Orthodox approach to prayer. I have been deliberately selective and have taken from these writings those ideas and insights that I have found to be particularly useful and have neglected others. For those who are interested, there is an appendix that lists the authors quoted and offers a brief comment about each of them.

The approach presented here, however, is not mainly derived from books. It arises largely from my own experience and from what I have learned of the experience of others; it is the result of my own exploration. People are all different, not least in the matter of how they pray. Anyone who has had the privilege of hearing from other people something of their experience of their own inner life and their awareness of God will realize just how different we all are. It is a mistake to think that we can all go about the prayer of silence in the same way. Each of us who embarks on this type of prayer needs to find his or her own way, but we can learn from and be helped by others. It is possible as we go along to dialogue with one another, listening to each other's wisdom and experience. This book is an attempt to take part in such a dialogue.

It will be obvious to thoughtful readers that a discussion of silent prayer carries theological implications. I am not unaware of these, but a short book like this is not the place to discuss them. I have tried also to avoid theological jargon or specialized language having to do with spirituality, so as to make the book more accessible to the general reader.

Silent prayer is a single activity involving contact at a deep level with our inner selves and with God. It has many sides or aspects, but it is a single whole. It cannot properly be divided up into different stages or steps that follow one after another. But in writing about it one is obliged to discuss these aspects separately: it is impossible to talk or write about them all at once. The result is that the subject has to be divided up into different sections. I would ask the reader to bear in mind that no section stands by itself. If I discuss "Entering Oneself" in chapter 3, followed by "Encountering God" in chapter 4, I am not suggesting that these two aspects of silent prayer are separate and follow one another. They belong together as parts of a whole. Each chapter needs to be taken along with the others, including those that come after it, and I have found it necessary from time to time to return to points made earlier in a different context.

To pray in silence we need to take certain practical steps. Thus, in chapter 2 I offer some thoughts and suggestions about how we can go about it in practice. These steps are fairly elementary and may be bypassed by those who already have their own way of silent prayer. My main intention is to go beyond these practical questions and to describe and discuss what happens when we engage in silent prayer. The prayer of silence involves a process. What we experience in the course of this process—our experience of our inner selves and of the presence and absence of God—is something that cannot be described in words. Occasionally we may have extraordinary experiences, and these are unquestionably beyond the power of words to express. More often what happens within us is much more ordinary, perhaps even dull, but even this, because it is something hidden deep within us, cannot adequately be described. My intention in the book is not to try to capture and describe something that is beyond description but to attempt to point to it and to describe aspects of the process in such a way that those who already engage in the prayer of silence may be able to recognize something held in common; and those who have not approached prayer in this way may be encouraged to do so.

1

Silence:
A Mysterious Reality

For many people today silence is a rare and precious commodity. We live in a noisy, busy world where sounds of all kinds surround us and the demands of life press upon us. So it is not surprising that many people have a great urge to get away for a little while from the noise and bustle and enjoy some quiet and peace. But silence is not merely an escape from noise and bustle: it can be a means to something deeper, a way of entering into a special kind of prayer. The growing demand for retreats and quiet days suggests that many people are aware of this and are keen to use a time of silence for deepening their prayer.

Prayer is usually expressed in words, whether the formal words of liturgy, the words of prayers composed by other people, or our own words used to express our thoughts and feelings to God. But words are only the vehicle; the heart of prayer lies deeper. It is not the words that constitute prayer but something underlying them, the opening of our inner self to God. In silent prayer we attempt to move beyond words, to reach a point where we are simply standing quietly before God and being in his presence. It is true that even in this kind of praying words may pass through our minds and may perhaps be mouthed by our lips; but these are not the prayer itself, only a means to something deeper, an avenue leading to a place where we are simply placing ourselves before God in silence.

The prayer of silence is an attempt to be in touch with God. Where, then, do we find God? Obviously God is not to be located in one place or another; but as we attempt to be aware of him we can find ourselves looking in different directions. We can think of God as being "up there," in "heaven," above and beyond us. When we do this we find ourselves directing our prayer upward. Or we can think of God as "everywhere," in the world and life around us, filling all things. In that case we will be open to discovering him in the things of nature or in events that happen to us. Or we can have the sense that God is within us, found in the depths of ourselves or in our inner hearts, in which case we will turn our gaze inward, looking deep within ourselves in order to be in touch with him. These different approaches are not mutually exclusive: we can look for God in different ways at different times. Some people are more especially drawn to the God within, and it is this approach to God that I will be exploring here. The prayer of silence, as I see it, is a matter of going down—down into the depths of oneself—in the belief that God is present and at work deep within us. This is not to suggest that God is contained within our hearts or is to be found only there. But by going down into ourselves, we can first of all discover and acknowledge something of the true, inner self that is often hidden from us; and then by doing this we can open ourselves to the God who can be encountered there. This is the aim of the prayer of silence.

There is a long tradition of this kind of prayer in the Christian community, probably going back into Old Testament times. It has been the work of monastics and mystics and of men and women who have devoted their lives to nothing else, some of whom have given up everything and have gone away to the desert or some lonely place. But it is also the task and calling of many ordinary people, people who know within themselves that they need to reach out for a deeper reality than they can find in conventional religious practice; who are dimly aware of the mystery that is at the heart of themselves and beyond themselves and are drawn to open themselves to it; and who long for God and will not be satisfied until they find themselves closer to him. For them the prayer of silence is both necessary and richly rewarding.

At the same time it can be frustrating. This kind of prayer is not always easy, comfortable, or satisfying. Those who go in for it do so not because it is a pleasant and attractive option but because they feel they can do no other; they have an inner urge, and they have no choice. In the prayer of silence they engage with a God whom they cannot grasp but from whom they cannot escape; who will not show himself but whom they cannot avoid; who will not take them fully to himself but who will not let them go; who will not be wholly present but who will not go away. It is a task in which progress cannot be measured, and whose goal seems always beyond us, an investment with no quick returns. It is undertaken not only by saints or mystics but by ordinary people who are not especially good or holy or prayerful, who feel to the end that they are not very good at it and may frequently wonder why they are doing it at all. But they are people who know that if they are to be true to themselves and faithful to the God whom they can sometimes only dimly discern, they must pursue this road. And they discover as they proceed that, unexpectedly, there are real rewards, spells of sunshine, times when God is delightfully close and a sense that, perhaps in spite of themselves, they are being taken along the road and drawn closer to the mystery of God.

Different Kinds of Silence

I use the phrase "prayer of silence" partly because to pray in this way we need an atmosphere of silence both outside ourselves and within ourselves. But there is more to silence than that. It can also provide the content and substance of our prayer. It is not only the prerequisite or the means of prayer, but in a sense also the prayer itself. The prayer of silence consists simply in being silent, the very silence itself constituting the prayer. Strange as it may seem, this does not mean that prayer becomes vague or empty of content, but rather is something rich and pregnant with meaning and possibility. To understand this we need to reflect on the meaning of silence.

What then is silence? The dictionary defines it as "absence of sound," and that is how we usually think of it. Seen in this way, silence is something we ourselves can bring into being. By stopping the noise or cutting out the sound we can create or produce silence. This is what we have in mind when we talk of "being silent" or "keeping silence." It suggests that silence is something negative. When there is no sound, no noise of voices or traffic or music or wind, there is silence. It exists only when we have got rid of sound or noise.

But we can see silence in a different way, not as something we can produce or bring about by getting rid of sound, but as something that exists in its own right, a positive reality that is there without our making it. It is something deep and mysterious, which we can explore and enter. We don't need to create it; instead we can allow it and discover it. There are times and circumstances when we can easily recognize this, times when the world around us is quiet and there is no audible sound. For many people this may not happen very often, but probably we can all think of some special occasions when this was so.

It is perhaps in the world of nature that we can be most aware of the silence that is around us all the time. We can sense the silence that surrounds the grass as it grows, the trees as they point silently upward on a still day, and the rocks as they sit solidly on the earth. If we take a walk in the country on a peaceful day, we can sometimes feel ourselves enveloped in a silence so profound that the sound of our footsteps on the path seems an intrusion and an offense. If we climb a hill and sit for a while on a lonely rock quietly listening, we can sometimes become aware of a silence so deep that we can "hear" it. We can sense a reality that is there, enfolding us, wrapping around us, until we are a part of it. This is the silence of the wide-open spaces, and we can listen to it. But we can be aware of the reality of the silence around us in other ways as well—for example, during an orchestral concert. Just at the point when the orchestra stops and before the eruption of the applause, there is often a precious moment of stillness, a few brief, fleeting seconds of rich, vibrant, almost tangible silence. It is not something produced by the orchestra or something artificially created. We sense it as a basic reality, a deep underlying silence that has been there all the time. The sounds of the music have themselves arisen out of it, have soared above it, and then have sunk back into it, and for a few brief seconds we can feel ourselves enfolded in it.

Silence is a reality that we can be aware of beyond or beneath the sounds that surround us. It has a substance that we can sometimes feel, a quality we can sense, a presence that is about us all the time, even though we often don't realize it. It is not something negative. It is a primary reality that exists beneath us and around us, but that gets hidden and overlaid by noise. All sound is set against the background of this primordial silence, arising out of it and dropping back into it. Silence has a depth and a mysterious quality that cannot be analyzed but can sometimes be expressed by poetry. We may recall Walter de la Mare's description of a horseman riding off into the night and of how, when the sound of the horse's hoofs had died away, the silence "surged softly backwards." The silence was there all along. It was pushed into the background by the intruding sound, but when this was gone it surged back again like an enveloping wave.

This, of course, is poetry, in the world of imagination. But it expresses the fact that, although much of the time silence is overlaid, crowded out, or chased away by noise, it is nevertheless still around us as a deep reality. It has its own special quality and can be experienced as a vibrant presence. This is the situation most of us are in most of the time: we are surrounded by sounds of various kinds that overlay and crowd out the silence. But, as we shall see, even in this situation we can train our ears and our minds to recognize and listen to the silence that is still there underneath the noise.

This silence that is all around us is not, however, the only kind of silence. It is the physical counterpart of two other, more hidden forms. There is a silence within us, at the inner center of ourselves, that is something deeper, more mysterious, and more difficult to identify. Beneath our conscious and unconscious mental activity, beneath the turmoil of our minds and feelings, at the center of our inner selves, there is a place of stillness and quietness, a still point in our turning world. This is the silence not of the wide-open spaces but of the deep pool. There are depths within us that we cannot fathom, that seem to have no bottom, and in these depths, at the very heart of ourselves, there is a profound silence. We are not usually aware of it. Most of the time our minds are active; we are occupied with thoughts and intentions of all kinds and are moved by a variety of feelings and impulses. All of this is noise that obscures our silent depths. Even more than the silence around us, the silence within us is overlaid and covered up by a constant hubbub of mental activity. The surface of the pool is disturbed and muddied by the busyness of our minds. But deep below this activity, below the rippling surface, there is quietness; and if we attend to it and learn how to listen to it, we can begin to "hear" it.

There is yet another kind of silence, something more profound and mysterious still—the silence of God. We are used to the idea that God "speaks." We think of our contact with God as taking place largely through words—our words spoken to him, and his word addressed to us. But God's word itself arises out of silence. What we call God's word is his communication to human beings, expressed in part in the form of human words; but this is not his being or essence. God's being is beyond all words. It is a mystery that human thought cannot grasp or language describe, which we can only faintly discern, but it can be represented by silence. "God is silence," says Abraham of Nathpar, "and in silence is he sung and glorified."[1] Behind God's spoken word, at the heart of God himself, there is a silence that enshrouds the deep mystery of God. There is no adequate analogy to this mystery. We may say that this is the silence not of the wide-open spaces of nature, nor of the deep pools of water, but of the distant stars and the far-flung universe. But even this metaphor falls short and collapses before the mystery of the silence of God. It is not a silence that we can "hear," like the silence of the world around us; but we can dimly sense it and be drawn toward it. There is a strange connection between this silence and the silence at the heart of our inner selves, a reciprocal relation that no metaphor can adequately express, a wonderful exchange between us and God through the medium of silence. Our silence, we may say, "echoes" the unspoken silence of God, reaches out to it and is enfolded in it. In a mysterious way God communicates with our inner heart through his silence.

These different kinds of silence are not disconnected and separate: they connect with each other and can lead into one another. It is this that makes the prayer of silence possible and forms its basis. The silence of the world around us connects with the deeper silence of our hearts, and this connects with the mysterious silence of God. It is in this way that silence becomes not just a prerequisite for prayer but prayer itself. As we learn to listen to and enter the silence that underlies the noise that usually surrounds us, we find we can go down into the pool of silence that lies within us; and this in turn leads us into the deep silence of God. One form of silence draws us on and down into the next. As St. Isaac of Nineveh said, "Out of this silence something is born that leads to silence itself."[2] It is through being drawn into these deeper forms of silence that we engage in silent prayer.

Another way of expressing this is to say that silence is sacramental. If a natural object or some aspect of the life of the world has the power to point beyond itself and lead us to God, it can be called "sacramental." This can be said, for example, of holy places or of some kinds of art and music.

Some of these may reflect some particular aspect of the character of God and may make that real for us in a way that words cannot express. Silence is one such thing. When the natural silence of the world around us draws us down to the silence within us, this in turn leads us sacramentally to the deep silence of God and points us toward the mystery of his being.

Love Silence

Engaging in the prayer of silence involves making a practice of entering this silence. As we do so, we come to treasure and cherish it. We discover that it can flow over and enfold us, like the warmth of a heated room on a cold winter day. We find that it is full of potential and possibilities, that it is the seedbed for the development of our inner life. That is not to say that it is always pleasant and comforting, for it has a darker side as well. For those who are constantly surrounded by noise it may at first seem strange and lonely, and perhaps even frightening. As we shall see, entering the silence both around us and within us can at times be unnerving. But as we persevere, it becomes something that we love, because it leads us toward the rich fruit of a deeper and more fulfilling relationship with God, which our tongues cannot express. As Isaac of Nineveh said, "Love silence above all things because it brings us close to the fruit which the tongue cannot express."[3]

Grant me, Lord…that converse which praises you in silence, you the Silent One who are praised in ineffable silence.

(Anonymous Syrian writer)[4]

I offer to you…the worship that befits you, O glorious God who dwells in ineffable silence.

(Isaac of Nineveh)[5]

The lover of silence draws close to God.

(John Climacus)[6]

Blessed is the mind that keeps perfect silence in prayer.

(St. Nilus of Sinai)[7]

This silence is the absorption of all the powers of a human being: they are all drawn towards God, and as it were disappear before His endless majesty.

(Theophan the Recluse)[8]

Silence is receptivity. It makes us attentive and allows a conversation with God that goes beyond words.

(Olivier Clément)[9]

2

Finding a Way:
Some Practical Steps

"There are as many kinds of prayer as there are different states of soul, as many kinds of prayer as there are souls." This was the conclusion reached by John Cassian,[1] a monk who had had conversations with the Desert Fathers. Some prayer is spoken in words, and some is silent and wordless. Both kinds are important: they complement and supplement each other and need not be entirely separated. Many people find it useful to approach the prayer of silence by means of a daily office or through their own words addressed to God, and they discover that verbal prayer can lead on into silence. But this will not suit everyone. We need to work out for ourselves how best we can combine and balance our silent and our spoken prayer.

When it comes to silent prayer and how we go about it, here too we all need to discover and develop a way that is appropriate for us. We need to pay attention to such matters as how we arrange our times of prayer and whether there are methods or techniques that can help us. In all these matters people are different. What follows in this chapter is not a set of rules, or even of guidelines, but a number of simple basic thoughts and practical suggestions, drawn from my own experience and the wisdom of others, which may help in the process of discovering our own way. It should be emphasized at the start, however, that practical steps are not important in themselves. The prayer lies not in the method but in our openness to God and in his drawing near to us. Methods and practical steps are important only insofar as they help toward this end.

Time and Place

The prayer of silence requires time. Most of us cannot go deeply down into silence in a few snatched minutes: we need a period of unhurried and unpressured time. For many people who live busy lives it isn't easy to find the time that is needed, and we have to work out for ourselves how we can do this. Just how much time we need will vary from one person to another. Everyone who tries to pray in any way also knows that certain times suit one better than others. At some times of day we tend to be more alert, and at other times more sluggish. There are occasions when we are cluttered up and preoccupied with all our daily concerns. Many of us, of course, have little choice. The demands of work, family, daily life, and bodily needs will dictate when time can be made available for prayer. But, generally speaking, insofar as we have any choice in the matter, we should pray at a time when we are mentally alert but not caught up in other things. For some this means the early morning, before the business of the day takes over. Like the lark, they can rise early and soar upward in the freshness of the morning. Others find themselves too sluggish in the morning and prefer to stay up late like the owl, keeping vigil in the quietness of the end of the day. Here again we each have to discover our own needs and opportunities.

We also need a pattern, an arrangement by which we try to pray at the same time each day or each week. The prayer of silence is not a static thing, but something that develops and grows and becomes deeper as we continue with it. For this to happen we need to engage in it regularly and consistently, not occasionally or casually. It needs to become part of the rhythm of life, in the same way as eating or sleeping, something we do routinely, not sporadically. Such an arrangement is often called a "rule," but this can bring difficulties. Some people who try to observe a rule feel themselves duty-bound to keep it every day no matter what else is going on. When inevitably they sometimes fail to follow their rule, they have a feeling of guilt that drags them down. Rules can also be unrealistic and overambitious. It is easy for some people to become rule-bound, to be more concerned with keeping the rule than with praying. It is worth heeding the advice of a Russian spiritual director known as Father John: "With regard to your rule of prayer, arrange it yourself, but in such a way that meaning is not lost for the sake of completing the rule.... I advise you not to take on much, so as not to be a slave to the rule."[2] Prayer should be freeing not binding, and we need to avoid the kind of rule-keeping that leaves us carrying around a load of guilt. Nevertheless, most of us do need a pattern that we try to observe in a disciplined way, a rhythm of prayer that fits naturally into the rhythm of the rest of our lives; and we need to find time for this.

There is, however, one time that has a special quality—the night. This is a time that has always had a special significance for some people of prayer. The Psalms show us that men and women in Old Testament times attached importance to the night as a time for calling on God. Jesus also used this time, sometimes spending the whole night in prayer. Ever since, monastics and hermits, especially in the Christian East, have preserved the tradition of vigil and prayer in the night. Isaac of Nineveh writes: "Let every prayer that you offer in the night be more precious in your eyes than all your activities of the day."[3] Keeping night vigil, he believed, was "a work filled with delight." Such night prayer or vigils were especially the work of the monastics and solitaries for whom Isaac was writing; but even today, many ordinary people who find themselves awake during the hours of darkness use the time for prayer. For most people, of course, the night is simply for sleep. But those who are wakeful during the night can discover in it an opportunity for silence of a special kind. The "wee small hours" in the dead of night are a mysterious time. The darkness, the stillness, and the state of our bodies and minds lend to this time an air and character all of its own, pregnant with a silence that is unique. It can be a time when God seems especially near, or when the "demons" of worry or fear are particularly present. Sometimes the night is fearful, invaded by disturbing thoughts and fantasies; and sometimes it is peaceful and open to thoughts of God. Either way, it is a time that some people find especially good for welcoming and using silence. Clearly, this does not suit everyone. But for the "night watchmen," the "owls" who wake in the night, this can be a special time of silent prayer, which can be built into their rhythm of praying.

For the prayer of silence we need also an appropriate place. For many it is helpful to be alone. Solitude is an important element in the prayer of silence. Solitude, of course, is not just a matter of being physically alone—it has an inner and deeper dimension, about which we will speak later—but physical solitude can help to lead us into silence.

Jesus, we are told, went off to a "lonely" or solitary place to pray, and the desert has always been important both practically and symbolically in the Christian spiritual tradition. There is a long history of hermits and solitaries who have gone to the deserts of Egypt or Palestine, to islands off the shores of Britain or Ireland, or to some other isolated place to be alone with God in silence. Even those of us who live in the world often find that solitude deepens silence. Sometimes we may have the opportunity to go to a lonely place out of doors where we can spend some time quietly all by ourselves. More often we will find our solitude simply in our own room with the door firmly shut. Once again people's needs are not all the same. For some it is helpful to be with other people, perhaps in a silent prayer group, where the sense that others are engaged in the same thing draws them down into silence. But for many, solitude has a special quality. The sense that there is no one else about, that we will not be distracted by the presence or the sounds of another person, and that we can be utterly alone with God can make it easier to go down into silence and to feel its mysterious depths. To quote Isaac of Nineveh again: "We have need of seclusion, that we may have the possibility the more readily to converse with God."[4]

It is also a help if we can find a quiet place where there is no disturbing noise. For this reason, retreat houses are usually situated in peaceful places in the country, and quiet days are held in some peaceful spot. For day-to-day purposes, when we can't take ourselves to a special place of silence, it is a help to find a place where there is little noise. If we can go into our room and shut the door, as Jesus directed, or go off to some quiet place outside where we will be undisturbed for a while, as Jesus himself did, we find it easier to be aware of the silence that lies below everything and to allow ourselves to be drawn into it.

By choosing the right time and place we can try to create conditions of quiet. Even when we do this, however, we may not be totally successful. In the world of today many people find it very difficult to escape from distant, background, or occasional noise of one kind or another. Often when we take time for prayer we do not get away altogether from ambient sound, however slight. The noise of traffic or machinery, of someone's radio, or of people's voices in the distance keeps intruding on our quietness. More importantly, even a quiet place does not get rid of the more disturbing kind of noise— the sound of what is going on within us. The chatter of thoughts in our head and the buzz and clamor of our feelings can be louder than the sounds outside us. I shall turn later to the question of what to do with this noise within us, but for the moment I will suggest that there are certain practical steps that can help us to be aware of the silence that under-lies both the noise around us and the disturbance within, and to open ourselves to it.

Stillness of Body

We need to start by making our bodies still. This means, first of all, making our tongues still, especially at the time of prayer but to some extent at other times as well. If we are in the habit of always being involved in talk, in a ceaseless to-and-fro of conversation, we will find it hard, when we want to pray, to enter into silence.

Then we need to make the rest of our body still. The body is important in prayer of all kinds. Being bodily creatures, we can express a great deal by our gestures, our postures, and our movements. Nowadays we are all conscious of body language in relationships. Our gestures, the expressions on our faces, the way we hold and move our bodies, all these are part of our communication with other people. Body language is also a part of our relationship with God. By the posture we adopt and by the signs and gestures we make we can express our attitude toward God. At a time when people were more conscious of social position and rank than we are today, they used their bodies to express respect, deference, or even veneration toward other human beings. In the presence of kings and emperors people bowed or prostrated themselves. Similarly, when we are aware of the presence of God, we express our worship and adoration partly through our bodies, by kneeling or standing, bowing our heads, joining or raising our hands. When we pray we need to adopt a physical posture that makes it easy to remember the presence of God and that expresses our humbling of ourselves before God's mystery. A casual or slovenly posture does not convey a sense of reverence. The practice of kneeling for prayer is a natural one, going back to Old Testament times, but there are other ways of expressing reverence. In the Orthodox tradition people normally express their reverence by standing to pray and sometimes by prostrations, deep bows, and the sign of the cross.

For the prayer of silence our bodies can help or hinder our concentration and stillness. In the words of Mark the Ascetic, one of the early Egyptian Fathers, "The mind cannot become silent without the body."[5] Since praying in silence may involve a fairly long period of time and require a special degree of concentration, it is important to assume a posture in which our bodies are both relaxed and alert. If some part of our body is drawing attention to itself because it is uncomfortable, this becomes a distraction from our prayer. But if we are too comfortable we may find concentration difficult—and we may be more inclined to sleep than to pray! What precise posture we adopt will vary from one person to another. Some find that the practice of sitting with a straight back is helpful. But for the approach to silent prayer presented here, which is based on going down into the heart, it may be more important to bow one's head, both out of reverence for God and in order to focus on one's heart. This can be done while using a kneeling stool or while sitting upright on a chair. The school of Orthodox monks known as hesychasts (that is, people of silence or stillness) used to engage in long periods of silent prayer sitting on a low stool with their head and shoulders bowed, and their chin resting on their chest in order to concentrate on their physical heart. Some even followed the example of the prophet Elijah in 1 Kings (18:42) and put their head between their knees! Whatever position we adopt, we should try to ensure that our bodies can remain as far as possible motionless for the time of our prayer, in a posture that both expresses our reverence and assists our concentration.

Attention

Having adopted our posture for prayer, we are then in a position to focus our minds and attention. For the prayer of silence we need to turn our attention away from other things that have been occupying it and calm or quiet the whirl of thoughts and feelings circulating in our heads. We can do this in part by listening. I suggested in the previous chapter that it is possible to listen to silence. It is not hard to do this when we are in a very quiet place, but even when there are sounds around us we can recognize that there is a silence beneath them that links with the silence of our inner selves and the silence of God. We can train our ears to reject or ignore external sounds and to listen to silence wherever we are. We are all familiar with the kind of situation where many people in a room are all talking together, but we are having a conversation with one of them. We find that our ears can select the voice of the person that we want to listen to and let all the others recede into the background. In the same way we can learn to select out the silence from among all the ambient sounds and listen only to that. This may take some time. The surrounding noises may only gradually lose their salience and obtrusiveness and fade away. But if we allow time for it we find that our ears do in fact select the silence that is there all the time and we can listen to it. By doing this we can be led into the deeper silence that is the ground of our silent prayer.

We need then to concentrate on our heart. As we shall see, the *heart*—in the sense of our spiritual heart, our inmost self—is the seat of our prayer; and the prayer of silence involves descending into this inner heart. We are helped to do so by focusing our attention on the physical heart, the body's engine tucked away in our chest. We are bodily creatures, and we can escape from the distractions and abstractions of our heads by going down into our bodies. For this, our eyes can be either a help or a hindrance. If under our closed eyelids our eyes move to and fro, our minds will probably follow them. But it is possible, even when our eyes are shut, to direct them downward into our chest, toward our heart. If with closed eyes we can gaze inward and peer into the darkness within, we can draw our attention away from our heads, reduce our roving mental activity, and help our minds to be still.

As we become more still and focused, we become conscious of our breathing. Most of the time the silent movement of air in and out of our bodies goes on without our being aware of it. Making ourselves conscious of it aids the prayer of silence in more than one way. In the first place it helps to make us still. The regularity of the movement as our breath goes in and out has a calming and quieting effect. As we become aware of this movement we find the whirl of other thoughts beginning to recede and die away. Along with this, consciousness of our breathing helps us to go down into ourselves. The air we breathe goes down inside us: we can feel it going into our chest, carrying oxygen to our lungs and heart. When we focus on this intake of breath, our attention is drawn downward into our heart. If we then make a point of breathing more deeply, filling our lungs more fully, we find ourselves taken more deeply down into ourselves. Some people may also find it helpful, in the course of a spell of silence, to slow down the movement of their breathing a little, pausing for a few seconds after breathing out and creating a moment of absolute stillness and emptiness before the next intake of air. The great hesychast writer Gregory Palamas suggests that "even beginners" can be taught not only "to introduce the mind within through breathing" but also "to restrain their breath somewhat, so that, together with their breath, they may hold the mind inside."[6] The little space between breaths further deepens our stillness and makes us more aware of our inner self.

The physical activity of breathing then comes to have a deeper significance. As our breathing slows down, we become aware of our dependence on our breath for life itself.

And this can remind us that it is God who gives the breath of life. In both Greek and Hebrew, the words for "breath" *(pneuma* and *ruah)* also mean "spirit." In the Genesis story it was when God breathed into the first human being that "the man became a living being" (Gen 2:7). It is the breath or Spirit of God within us that gives us life, so our breathing represents God's Spirit breathed into us. It is not just a physical activity but a means of being open to God and receiving him into ourselves. As we take in air, we take into ourselves also the life-giving Spirit of God. Breathing then becomes a part of our prayer. In the words of the influential Russian spiritual guide Theophan the Recluse, "Just as in breathing the oxygen is received into the blood and then distributed to bring life to the body, so in prayer, what is received from God enters our innermost being and gives new life to everything there."[7]

Rhythm Prayer

For many people, awareness of breathing goes along with the use of a rhythm prayer. By this is meant a very short prayer consisting of only a few words that are repeated over and over again, along with one's breathing. The slow repetition of a rhythm prayer can help us in a number of ways. It can combine with our breathing to produce a sense of stillness and calm. This should not be done as a kind of mechanical technique. Instead it should be, in the words of another Russian spiritual writer, Bishop Ignatii, "an unhurried repetition of the prayer, a brief pause after each prayer, quiet and steady breathing, and enclosing the mind in the words of the prayer."[8] As we draw the air into our lungs by our deep breathing, we draw down the words of the prayer into our hearts, so that they become not just empty words, nor simply the thoughts of our heads, but a vehicle for the desires and feelings of our hearts.

Repeating a rhythm prayer also helps us to deal with distractions—a constant problem to which I shall return shortly. It does so in two ways. Slow repetition of the prayer in time with our breathing helps us to move out of our heads into our hearts and so calms and quiets the whirl of our thoughts. As we settle into the gentle rhythm of the prayer, the concerns of our minds move farther away and we become more still. In addition, the words of the prayer can become the focus of our attention. If the words are addressed to God, they can help us to give our attention only to him.

A rhythm prayer is more than just a technique for stillness; it is a prayer in the sense of something that helps us to be nearer God. In the Orthodox tradition it usually takes the form of the Jesus Prayer: "Lord Jesus Christ, Son of God, have mercy on me," sometimes with the addition "a sinner." This is based most directly on the prayer of the publican in Jesus' parable of the Pharisee and the publican in Luke 18; but the plea for God's mercy is found in many places in the Psalms and the Gospels and is echoed in the *"Kyrie eleison"* ("Lord, have mercy") of the church's liturgy. Its importance for many people lies in its use of the name of Jesus. The prayer invokes the power of the Name to bring us the help and healing of God. In this way, the Jesus Prayer is more than a formula; within the Orthodox tradition, it is a central part of a disciplined way of life and prayer. But even within that tradition other forms of rhythm prayer are possible. Theophan the Recluse commends standing before the Lord with the Jesus Prayer "or with any other words," acknowledging that "it is one amongst various short prayers." "The

power is not in the words but in the thoughts and feelings."⁹
Some of the early monks of Egypt and Palestine used the
opening of Psalm 70, "O God, make speed to save me; O
Lord make haste to help me," and others simply repeated the
common biblical petition "Lord, have mercy." Among people
today, a great variety of forms of the rhythm prayer are in
use. I suggest adapting another liturgical form, the Trisagion,
and saying, "Holy God, have mercy on me." Generally
speaking, the words of a rhythm prayer should express both
our sense of the greatness of God and our awareness of our
own personal need of his help and mercy. To some this may
seem too individualistic, too centered on oneself. But the
more fully we enter into this plea for mercy, uttered from the
depths of the heart, into which we are drawn by our silence,
our breathing, and our rhythm prayer, the more we recognize
that to stand helpless and powerless before God calling for
his mercy is the starting point of all our praying. This is the
basis of our petitions for ourselves and for other people. All
our other prayers can grow from this.

A rhythm prayer has one other important aspect: it can
be used anywhere, at any time. We can repeat it quietly at
any moment of the day or night, whenever our mind is free.
It can even become a means of "unceasing prayer," a way of
fulfilling in a literal sense St. Paul's injunction to "pray without ceasing" (1 Thess 5:17). The well-known Russian story
"The Way of the Pilgrim" explains how, by deliberately
repeating the Jesus Prayer many thousands of times, a young
man found that it had "entered his heart," that it was being
repeated deep within him all the time even when he was not
aware of it. To some extent we can all share this experience.
If we use a rhythm prayer often enough, repeating it over
and over in our periods of silence and at any other given

opportunity, we find it returns spontaneously to our minds or lips, or that it reverberates in our hearts, at all sorts of times, and we begin to move toward unceasing prayer.

Distractions

Most people find that while they are at prayer their thoughts wander. We try to focus on God and suddenly we find that our mind has gone off onto something else. I have already suggested that we can reduce this by concentrating on our breathing and by using a rhythm prayer; but for most of us the problem still remains. Some people are inclined to feel that this is their own peculiar weakness, and they tell themselves that they are "just not very good at prayer." The truth is that we are not alone in this. It is an experience shared by the great contemplatives and mystics. John Cassian, relaying the experience of the Desert Fathers, says: "This is what happens in fact. Our thoughts wander from spiritual contemplation and run hither and thither."[10] Writing from within a different spiritual tradition, Teresa of Avila complains: "I cannot endure this wandering of the mind!"[11]

There have been many suggestions about how to deal with these distractions. Teresa adopts a typically light-hearted approach: "When one of you finds…[that] the thought wanders off…she should laugh at it, and treat it as the silly thing it is, and remain in her state of quiet."[12] Others have suggested that we should learn to ignore the distracting thoughts and let them drift past. The great Syrian monk known as Pseudo-Macarius reminds us that our distractions are in fact our thoughts, which have originated in us. They are, he says, our "straying children" that have been "scattered abroad." What we need to do is not chase them away but rather gather them together back into our inner selves. "Let the soul lead them into the home of its body."[13]

Whatever we do with them, distracting thoughts will persist. This is only natural, especially at the start of our period of silence. The process of making ourselves still and going down into our heart is for most of us a slow one. We can't expect that our wandering thoughts will be gathered together immediately and our minds be stilled all at once. We need to allow time for this. That is not to say that after some time has passed all distractions will cease; we may find our mind wandering at any point. But if we take adequate time for our praying, attend to our posture and our breathing, and use our rhythm prayer, we may find ourselves drawn downward to a deep inner place where the noises in our heads are stilled and the distracting thoughts are put to rest, and we can remain for a few moments in the deep silence of prayer.

Perseverance and Grace

From all this it will be clear that the prayer of silence is not easy. It requires both effort and perseverance. Those who engage in it seriously find that it is hard work. Even when we make the effort, we find that our time of prayer is not always enjoyable. Sometimes we feel it "does nothing for us" and is pointless. We may find that our waiting for God turns into waiting for the time of prayer to end! If we are to continue with it, it requires perseverance, the willingness to go on even when it seems to do no good. But if we persevere, we find that, although it is not always apparent at the time, our times of silent prayer do bear some fruit within our inner self and that gradually we are changed. The value of the prayer of silence is revealed not on any one occasion but over a longer period. We probably also discover, as we continue the practice of praying in this way, that by the end of our times of prayer we increasingly have a sense of reaching the depths, of being taken beyond ourselves, of being held by God, and of having a part in a wonderful exchange. We may also from time to time have a sense of still more marvelous gifts, the wonder of being enfolded in the mystery, the thrill of the near presence of God, the comfort and warmth and reassurance of his grasp, or some other experience that we cannot describe in words.

The important thing about the prayer of silence, however, is not our effort or perseverance. Although some practical steps, such as those I have described, may be necessary, they do not constitute the prayer. We need not concern ourselves too much about the effects or results of our silent prayer. What we receive through our prayer, and indeed the prayer itself, is all the gift of God. We do need to bring effort and perseverance to our prayer, but the purpose of this is simply to enable us to be open to the working of God within us. Whatever we receive through prayer is the result not of our efforts but of the grace of God. When a person prays, says Theophan, "God it is who prays in him...God it is who bears the fruit in him."[14]

When all has been said about methods and practical steps, the task of silent prayer remains essentially a very simple one. It consists in placing ourselves before God and waiting before him in silence. The deeper aspects of the prayer of silence all flow from this.

[Inner prayer] is performed when you are alone in the shut closet.... The material closet remains always in the same place, but the spiritual one you carry about with you wherever you go.

(St. Dimitri of Rostov)[15]

When at prayer a hesychast concentrates his look, his attention, on his physical heart.... By doing this, he becomes conscious of the center of his personal life.

(Elisabeth Behr-Sigel)[16]

Breathing is a natural way to the heart.

(Nicephorus the Solitary)[17]

The Spirit is the hidden God, the inward God, deeper than our greatest depth. He gives life to all things and we breathe him without being aware of it.

(Olivier Clément)[18]

If one concentrates on it [a rhythm prayer] with zeal, it will begin to flow of its own accord, like a brook that murmurs in the heart.

(Theophan the Recluse)[19]

God does not demand of those under obedience that their thoughts be totally undistracted when they pray. And do not lose heart when your thoughts are stolen away. Just remain calm, and constantly call your mind back.

(John Climacus)[20]

3

Entering Oneself:
A Secret Place

The prayer of silence has a double aspect: entering ourselves and encountering God. These are two inseparable parts of the single activity of prayer, representing two sides of a reciprocal relationship. Although they belong together, something should be said about each of them, and so I will discuss them separately, in this chapter and the next.

Descending to the Heart

Silent prayer is not simply a matter of taking some practical steps: it is an inner process that takes place deep within us. So we need to start by entering our inner selves. Strange as it may seem, although God is beyond us and infinitely greater than we are, we reach out to him not by looking far into the beyond but by going down into what has often been called our "inner chamber." Jesus said, "Whenever you pray, go into your [inner] room and shut the door" (Matt 6:6). This "inner room" may be taken to refer not simply to a physical room but to our inner selves, our secret inner chamber. It is by going down into this secret place within us that we can relate to God in prayer. "Strive to enter within your inner chamber," said Isaac of Nineveh, "and you will see the chamber of heaven."[1]

This inner chamber is our heart. The importance of focusing our attention on our physical heart, in the way described in the previous chapter, is that this helps us to enter our spiritual heart. Used in the biblical sense, the "heart" refers not simply to our feelings or emotions but to the inner core of our personality, the seat and mainspring of our thoughts and feelings. The heart is our essential self, the inmost center of ourselves, which no one else can enter and where we know ourselves to be "Me." It is the place from which our thoughts, feelings, and motives—and, therefore, our actions—arise. It is down into this inner place that we must go if we are to engage in silent prayer. "Our heart is the root and center of life," says Theophan; and in order to pray we must descend into the heart.[2]

Or, to put this in another way, we need to put our "mind in our heart." That is to say, our attention must be focused not on what is going on in our heads but on our inner center. We need to move out of our heads into our hearts. The head is the place of thought and rational activity, the place where we are aware of external things. In our heads there is usually a turmoil of thoughts, often driven along by a variety of emotions. When our attention remains centered on what is in our heads, we are caught up in one way or another with the world around us, and it is impossible to engage in silent prayer. "The head," says Theophan, "is a crowded rag-market: it is not possible to pray to God there."[3] John Climacus uses even stronger imagery, calling the mind that stays in the head a "cur sniffing around the meat market and reveling in the uproar"![4] To engage in silent prayer we need to move out of this busy market and go down into the place of stillness deep within us. With the help of some of the practical techniques I have already described, we can reach below the chatter of our thoughts and the turmoil of our emotions and enter our heart.

Our heart is the place of prayer, the place where our inner silence links us with the silence of God. It is a place of mysterious depth. Some people experience their heart as bottomless, something like a shaft or a cavern within themselves into which they can gaze but which they cannot fathom. The practice of the prayer of silence involves penetrating further and further into the mystery of this inner self. As we continue with this kind of prayer we find ourselves entering depths we had not encountered before, and discovering a part of ourselves we did not know existed. Here words are no longer required. That is not to say that they can play no part. Although the prayer of silence is wordless, words can sometimes be used to carry our attention out of our head into the heart. The words of a rhythm prayer, or other phrases or verbal expressions that may come to us in the stillness can point us to the inner place that is beyond words and help us to penetrate further into the inner silence of our hearts. It is this silence, not the words that have helped to lead us into it, that is the medium of our prayer.

Our heart is also our feeling self, the place where we feel. Feeling—that is, the capacity to feel—is to be distinguished from feelings or emotions. The emotions are what we feel, the fluctuating feelings of sadness or happiness, anger or excitement, which vary with our circumstances or moods. Some of these are superficial and transient feelings, which may be a hindrance to prayer, as we shall see, but which can also find expression in prayer. Others are more deep-seated feelings, some of which can play an important part in the prayer of silence. The heart, however, should not be equated with our feelings: rather it is the organ of feeling, the "I" that senses and feels these feelings. It is the affective element at the core of ourselves, the part of us that can be moved, our sensitive, vulnerable center. For the purposes of prayer we need to descend below our superficial emotions into the heart. Here in our feeling center we can be open to more profound movements of feeling and so be more deeply open to God. Going down into this vulnerable core of ourselves, allowing ourselves to feel, and opening this feeling self to God are essential for silent prayer. "The principal thing in prayer," says Theophan, "is a feeling heart," a heart that is open to God so that we can "feel towards God."[5] We can then begin (in the words of Evagrius, one of the most seminal of early writers on prayer) "to pray with feeling."[6] For, in Olivier Clément's words, "God is felt by the feeling of the heart."[7] By descending into the heart we can allow the deep desire for God, which is the motive force for the prayer of silence, to grow within us. Here at the center of ourselves we can experience the longing for God that moves us to reach out to him in prayer.

Discovering Ourselves

This heart into which we can descend is our true self, and to enter it is to begin to discover that true self. Sadly, this self is often hidden and unknown. It is hidden, of course, from other people and may in large measure be hidden from ourselves as well. Our inner self feels vulnerable, and we feel the need to protect it. We may have inner fears or painful feelings that we are afraid will be opened up if we go down into our hearts, and so we shut them off by remaining on the surface of ourselves. Our inner self is also liable to be hurt by the ways and words of other people; so during the course of life we learn to hide and protect it from them. We develop ways of presenting ourselves to the world outside by behaving in ways that people expect or that will impress or please or overawe them. Unconsciously we put on something of an act. We have a persona, a mask that hides our true self, and we pretend to be something we are not. We spend our energies, and perhaps our whole lives, trying to be the person that we feel we ought to be, or that we would like to be, or that we think others expect us to be. The result is that we are often unknowingly taken in by our own pretense and believe we are the kind of people we try to show ourselves to be. Our true inner self is often hidden, not only from other people but also from ourselves. The mask obscures the reality from us as well.

But this is not the whole truth. Even those who have developed the most convincing pretense, who identify themselves with their mask, often have a sense that there is something else underneath. However much our true self may be hidden from us, we probably have a sense that it is there. Many people are aware that there is an inconsistency, perhaps an inner conflict, between the person they present both to the outside world and to themselves, and the person they truly are. I expect there is in everyone, at some level of themselves, a desire to know and be true to themselves, a deep wish to be in practice the person they really are. Human beings have a yearning to find their true inner being.

It is by going down into our heart that we discover our true selves and come to know ourselves. "Until the soul is established with the mind in the heart," says Theophan, "it does not see itself."[8] By descending through the layers of thought and feeling that are on the surface and putting our mind in our heart, we begin to learn who we really are.

Strangely, this is not as easy as one might think. It is only when we have made a practice for a long period of going down into the heart and being there in the presence of God that we begin to know ourselves. This requires patience and determination. In the words of Father John, a twentieth-century Russian spiritual guide, "Nothing is so difficult as to know oneself."[9] Our true self is not revealed to us all at once; it becomes known to us only gradually. As we continue descending into the heart, layers of self-misunderstanding are peeled off, and we find ourselves drawn into an ever-deeper understanding of ourselves. We realize that, in some respects at least, we are not internally the kind of person we thought we were. We begin truly to know ourselves.

To know oneself is not the same as understanding something of our psychological makeup. There are various means of discovering the psychological type we belong to and thereby understanding more about the way we feel, react, and behave, and this can be very useful. But this is to understand oneself with one's head. True self-knowledge, on the other hand, is a matter of the heart. When we reach underneath the thoughts and feelings that dominate the mind, and with which we too easily identify ourselves, and descend to our inner self, we can observe the movements of our mind and feelings without being identified with them. Here knowing and being come together. It is by knowing ourselves that we are able to be our true selves; and by being ourselves we come to know who we truly are. This is important for our ordinary life and relationships. Insofar as we stop pretending to be something we are not we find ourselves more inwardly free, relaxed, and able to relate to other people in a more genuine way. But for the prayer of silence it is a basic necessity. We cannot present a false or unreal self to the God to whom all hearts are open and all desires known and from whom no secrets are hidden. In order to hold ourselves still before God we need to go down to the place where we are truly ourselves.

This true self may be seen as our original self, the person we were when we started out on the road of life. Perhaps we can have a sense of it by recalling our earliest memories and identifying with the little child we were at the start. Over the years there have been many accretions and developments. We have acquired knowledge, learned skills, and developed habitual ways of thinking and acting. We have gained possessions, formed relationships, and reached a position of some kind in the world. We have acquired, even if only in modest ways, a measure of power. Beneath all this, the self we originally were may have become submerged or forgotten; but it is still there.

To own this original self is to recognize our uniqueness. Since each individual person is a separate subject with his or her consciousness of self, no two human persons are the same. Each of us is a "one-of." When we descend into the heart we are made conscious that there is no other "Me," no one else who knows what it is like to be Me. There are millions of others who are like me, but throughout the history of the world there never has been another Me. I have been given a self, a heart that is unrepeatable, a distinct unique creation that has never occurred before and will never recur again. Because of this, this original self, this Me is infinitely precious. It is a unique gift of God, to be loved, respected, and cherished. To be this Me is a task given to no one else. It is the special vocation of each of us and a part of the purpose of our life to discover and be this unique person that God has made us to be.

Doing this does not make us self-important and inflated; on the contrary it leads us toward humility. When we discover our true selves we have to accept our basic powerlessness. Underneath the knowledge, skill, and power we need for living and acting in the world we find an inescapable inability to help ourselves. We cannot be all we would like to be, solve all our problems, control the behavior of other people, or extend our years beyond their given span. To accept this powerlessness is an act of humility, and it is only humility that makes it possible for us to be before God in silent prayer. As Olivier Clément says, "It is by the depths of the humble heart, and not by some conceited ascent"[10] that we rise to God.

Solitude

When I go down into the heart I find myself alone. The heart is a secret, hidden place that no one else can enter. Since it is the organ of feeling, no other person can reach into it and subjectively share my feelings. No one knows from the inside what my feelings feel like. I can tell other people about my inner pain or happiness, and I can hope that they will understand and sympathize. I can assume that, because human beings are all very similar and apparently share the same emotional makeup, other people's experience will be the same as mine. But in fact no other person can find a way into my heart and share my subjectivity. My inner subjective experience remains unique to me; it can be described but it cannot be shared.

Because of this, although it is the place where we discover the joy and freedom of being ourselves, the heart is also a lonely place. Some people experience this in an acute

way and find it hard to bear. For sensitive people the awareness of inner isolation can be intense and frightening. At
times the heart can feel like an empty darkness or an internal desert, a vacant land with no other person in sight.
Perhaps this is why some people are hesitant to go down into
their heart, preferring to stay on the surface, in the company
of other people.

But if we are to engage in silent prayer we need at times
to be alone. Solitude is an essential element in the prayer of
silence. There are, of course, different kinds of aloneness or
solitude. As we have already seen, physical solitude can be
important. It is often helpful to take ourselves to a place
where there are no other people around, whether it is a lonely
place in the country or simply our own room with the door
firmly shut. The value of such physical solitude is that it can
lead to a deeper kind of solitude; it can help us to go down to
the place where we are alone within ourselves. Those who
have never learned to be physically alone, who are uneasy in
a solitary place without other people, will have difficulty in
discovering and entering their own inner solitude. And solitude is the important thing. "Secure for yourself inner solitude," says Theophan. "You will have something better than
external seclusion if you retreat in this way within yourself."[11]
As we discover this we begin to love solitude. Times when we
are physically alone become precious because they lead us
into this inner hermitage of the heart.

To descend into the heart, of course, we do not always
need to be physically alone. If we have once discovered inner
solitude, we can carry it around with us and go down into it
even in the midst of a crowd. It is possible, says Olivier
Clément, "to walk in the hubbub of the city carrying the
silence of the mountains in one's heart."[12] In this inner solitude

we are alone in a special way. Here in this solitary place we are mentally far from other people and are not engaged in mental conversation or exchange with them. Here the chatter of our internal voices can be put to rest, and we can listen to the silence of our hearts and of God. Here it becomes possible, even if perhaps only very briefly, to retreat completely into ourselves, to enter fully into our own subjectivity, just to be Me and nothing else, and so to become capable, in the words of the contemporary Romanian writer Dumitru Staniloae, "of getting loose for a few moments in succession from the slavery of contents,"[13] of losing our persistent awareness of the thoughts in our mind. Here we are in the secret place of the Most High, hidden away from the turmoil of the world. Here we are alone with God.

As we shall see in the next chapter, it is in this solitary place that God encounters us. The place of inner solitude in the depths of our heart is our meeting place with God. This is the holy of holies, where mysteriously God makes himself present. This is not to deny what I said earlier that the heart can be a lonely and sometimes frightening place. For many people entering their inner solitude may involve pain, sometimes so great that they cannot face it. But many have also found that it is precisely in this place of loneliness and pain that God encounters them, and that, when they are able to face their inner isolation, they have discovered a joy alongside their pain and a companion in their loneliness.

It may be asked, Is this not all too exclusive and individualistic? Is the urge to be alone with God not simply selfish, making us narrowly concerned only with ourselves and God, isolated from other people and careless of their needs? This need not and should not be so. It is true that pursuing the way of silent prayer has been called the loneliest journey in the world, because it is undertaken in the secret part of ourselves that no other person can enter; but it is also a journey in which we are accompanied by countless others. In the depths of ourselves we know that others journey with us, entering their own solitude where they too are alone with God. If they cannot fully share our subjective experience, they are at least alongside us, our companions in the way of silence. What is more, the prayer of silence links us with the rest of humanity in another way. Each of us is not only a unique person but also another human being like all the others around us. We share one human nature, are shaped by the same visible and invisible forces, are subject to the same kinds of pressures and emotions, and behave in similar ways. At a deep level we are not only individuals but also one with all humanity. The Me we know ourselves to be is a part and a representative of the race of human beings. Because of this, our inner silence can open up a deep and meaningful way of intercession, as we shall see later on.

The Passions

The heart is our meeting place with God; but it is also host to a great variety of thoughts and feelings that make their home within us, motivate our behavior, and affect our relationships. Our hearts can be covered over by a great variety of secret feelings and half-hidden thoughts that prevent us from opening ourselves fully to God. So, one of the first requirements of silent prayer is that we should be honest with ourselves and examine our hearts. When we do so we discover, embedded within us along with the desire and longing for God, thoughts and feelings that come between us and God, that spoil or obstruct our relationship with him. The Greek Fathers referred to these as the "passions." By this they meant not only what we might call "passionate" feelings, such as strong emotions of desire or anger, but all those hidden emotional tendencies, ingrained subjective attitudes, deep-seated prejudices, and unrecognized motives that lie behind our behavior and condition our way of being in the world. Of course, not all of these are bad. All of us are moved by what we may call "good passions"—feelings of compassion and caring for others, a spirit of self-sacrifice and courage, and a love of things that are beautiful. But if these inner urges are turned in a negative direction, they become destructive passions that deflect us from our relation with God and prevent us from being our true and best selves. The Fathers believed that these "evil thoughts," as they were sometimes called, were "not something naturally implanted," as John Climacus put it,[14] but were caused by the working of evil within us. Maximus the Confessor, a seventh-century theologian and spiritual writer who had much to say about the passions, referred to them as "an unnatural movement of the soul"[15]—something that should not be there and that separates us from God.

The Fathers usually identified eight such passions, which Evagrius, who first listed them, named gluttony, lust, avarice, despondency, anger, listlessness, vainglory, and pride.[16] This list was drawn up long ago largely with monks in mind, and many of us today may feel that it does not adequately describe what goes on in us; but it was based on the experience of people of prayer and spiritual depth who had examined themselves and acknowledged the truth of what they discovered. These passions described the negative things that they found within their hearts. So we can use their list as a basis for a way of describing some of the "passions" that many of us can recognize in ourselves.

If we translate their words into modern language and concepts, we can draw up a list of passions that seems nearer to our own experience. I suggest that they can be divided into two groups. We can think of a group of five passions that are all different ways of trying to grasp at life and get what we can out of it. First, there is the desire to possess— the urge to get what we can for ourselves, the wish to have things not simply so that we can enjoy them with thankfulness but because we need them to make us feel better about ourselves and give us a sense of security. Along with this goes the desire to control—the wish to be in charge of what happens to us, to manipulate other people's behavior toward us and to have our own way, thus closing off the potential of the unforeseen. Third, there is the urge to gratify our senses in an excessive way, to overindulge in physical pleasures, perhaps to compensate for inner fears or inadequacies. Fourth, there is pride, in the sense of arrogance or superiority, the feeling that in one way or another we are better than other people and can look down on them; the deriving of pleasure from others' failings and from the sense that we are not as they are. Fifth, there is what in old-fashioned language is called vainglory, the love of our own reputation and the desire to be praised and admired. All of these represent a grasping or predatory approach to life, a belief that in order to live successfully we need to wring what we can out of it, to get things for ourselves and make things go our way.

A second group of four passions consists of feelings or attitudes that arise in us when we discover that in one way or another we are unable completely to control life to our advantage and our grasping at life is not being wholly successful. In these circumstances we can find ourselves moved by envy, a feeling of sadness and bitterness that we do not have the abilities, achievements, reputation, or possessions that others have. Closely related to this is resentment, which is a form of anger—not an outburst of angry emotion but a deep-seated, lingering, and often hidden feeling that we have not been given our due or that someone has been unjust to us. Next comes a spirit of despondency or discouragement, a feeling of negativity toward life that can lead to cynicism, hopelessness, or even despair. Finally, there is anxiety. Since we are unable completely to control life to our advantage and guarantee our security, we feel anxious about what is going to happen to us. At a deeper level, if we are uncertain about our identity and our worth, we can be anxious about our inner selves also.

Such a list may provide some people today with a useful basis for examining their own hearts. But people differ, and others may find that this particular list does not help them to understand what is going on in them. We need not adopt this or any other list, but we can all look deep within ourselves to discover our own passions, the kinds of feelings, motives, and attitudes that are found within us, and which overlay our hearts. When we do so, I expect that most people can recognize that there are two feelings of a more basic kind that underlie all the passions. The first is what the Greek Fathers called "self-love" *(philautia),* or the false love of self. There is, of course, a right and appropriate love of self, a proper valuing of ourselves and a recognition of our worth and dignity as human beings. But there is also a self-love that results in our being centered on ourselves and dominated by self-interest, which leads us to look at everything from the point of view of how it affects us. It is this that underlies all the passions. It is self-love that makes us try to promote and establish ourselves and casts us down when we don't succeed. According to Maximus the Confessor, "he who has self-love has all the passions."[17] The second feeling is something deeper and more basic still. Underlying even our love of self is fear—not the fear of anything external, but of loss of self, of nonbeing, of our own nothingness, of the great void beneath us into which we may sink. According to Maximus again, the cause of all the passions is "the hidden fear of death."[18] This fear of the great abyss of nothingness below us goes along with our love of self, and together they make us cling to ourselves, prompt us to grasp at life in order to sustain ourselves, and cast us down into despondency or arouse our anxiety when our self-promotion lets us down. The passions, whatever form they may take, are all the out-workings of this basic existential fear and this insidious love of self that lurk within us, often hidden and unrecognized.

This, then, is one way of describing the negative things within us. The passions are habitual modes of feeling and thought that come between us and our true selves and hinder our relationship with God. They are, in Olivier Clément's words, "blockages, usurpations, deviations that destroy the human being's basic desire."[19] What form they take and what kind of power they exercise over us will vary from one person to another, but they are common to all humanity. They are individual yet shared by all. They are part of our human condition. This fact has important implications for our prayer. It is our sense of oneness with other people through being subject to the same passions that can make the prayer of silence into a form both of confession and of intercession, as we shall see later on.

What can we do with these passions? Is it possible to overcome them and free ourselves from these ways of feeling and thinking, so that we have an unhindered relationship with God? An answer to this question must wait until we have thought about how we encounter God in the depth of our heart. For the moment we should simply note that the first step in dealing with the passions is to realize that they are there. This may not be easy, because, even when we begin to descend into our heart, we may not always recognize them. This is because they are often hidden and operate in secret and subtle ways. We can be proud or resentful or anxious without realizing it. Our love of self and our fear of death often go unrecognized. "Passion," says John Climacus, "is properly something that lies hidden for a long time in the soul and by its very presence takes on the character of a habit."[20] According to Pseudo-Macarius, "The world thrives on evil passions and is ignorant of this fact."[21] That is why we need to examine ourselves carefully and honestly, in order to discover our own passions.

Coming to know our passions is one result of the process of entering our inner selves, a process that is an essential part of the prayer of silence. By descending into our heart and entering our inner solitude we begin to know and to be our true selves. Here we discover both our longing for God and the passions that hinder our relationship with him. The prayer of silence then involves laying all of this before God, opening ourselves and all that is in us to him, and holding ourselves before him in stillness and expectation. It is not a matter of doing or saying anything, but of being—simply being who and what we are in the presence of God. It is by being in silence in this way, in the depth of our heart, that we put ourselves in a position to encounter God.

It is impossible for us to become reconciled and united with God if we do not first return to ourselves, as far as it lies in our power, or if we do not enter within ourselves.

(Nicephorus the Solitary)[22]

The ascent to heaven is connected with the descent into ourselves. The more we sink our attention deep into our soul, the more we find our secret heart.

Hierotheos Vlachos)[23]

He who knows himself knows God.

(Anthony the Great)[24]

Our Lord bids us, "When you pray, enter your chamber and close your door." What, then, is this chamber, if not the inner house of the heart, whose door is kept closed by humility, which abhors praise from men.... In this way...[we are] hidden away as though in some secret hiding place.

(Sahdona)[25]

Hidden prayer is for the hidden ear of God.

(Ephrem the Syrian)[26]

How should you order yourself inwardly so as to enjoy peace of soul? Secure for yourself inner solitude.... This is the true wilderness.

(Theophan)[27]

Passion...is the expression of an egotism which wants to make all things gravitate around it.... [Passions] are the thick wall put between us and God, the fog covering our nature made transparent for God.

(Dumitru Staniloae)[28]

Beware of the mother of evil—self-love...giving birth to the whole tribe of passions.

(Maximus the Confessor)[29]

4

Encountering God: Shared Subjectivity

Presence in the Heart

It is in the heart that we encounter God. That is not to say, of course, that he cannot be encountered in any other place; but the heart is in a special way the dwelling place of God's Holy Spirit, the place which God has chosen as his abode. I believe he is present in the hearts of all people; for although the sacrament of baptism provides a special opportunity for God to work in people's hearts, his grace and the operations of his Spirit are not restricted to those who have been baptized. As Theophan says, "He is not far from anyone.... Find a place in your heart, and speak there with the Lord. It is the Lord's reception room. Everyone who meets the Lord, meets him there; He has fixed no other place for meeting souls."[1] As we move down beyond our thinking minds into our hearts, so God "comes down" to meet us there. In the words of Olivier Clément, "The person, going beyond the borders of the intellect, meets the living God who also, in his love, 'goes out' of himself, leaves his inaccessible transcendence."[2] This brings about the mutual encounter between us and God.

How, then, do we encounter God or become aware of his presence in our hearts? We cannot do so by our own actions or decisions. It is not we who encounter God, but God who encounters us. We cannot control the presence of God or decide how or when we encounter him. Our part is to lay ourselves open to this encounter. We do this in the prayer of silence by attempting to lay aside our other concerns and trying to focus our attention as far as possible on God and on him alone. Of course, at other times we will bring our concerns to God in our prayers of other kinds—our thanksgivings, our confessions, and our petitions for ourselves and other people. But the prayer of silence is prayer for God's sake, not for ours; in it our thoughts, our devotion, our adoration, and our love are simply directed to him. Nor is it the kind of prayer in which we use our imagination. Our mind should be stripped of thoughts and images, in order to gaze on God.

By going down into our hearts, holding ourselves still, and concentrating our attention on God in this way, we can have a sense of his presence. At various times and in different ways, sometimes unexpectedly, God makes us aware that he is there. This does not happen in the same way for everyone: people's inner lives vary a great deal, and the experience of God's presence comes to them in a variety of ways. Some have a very vivid sense of God and are aware of his presence nearly every time they go down into themselves in silence. But I think it is likely that the majority of praying people have only an occasional and perhaps rather vague sense of him, and that during many, if not most, of their times of silent prayer they have to wait in silence without being given anything that they would call an experience of God.

As we go deeper into the prayer of silence, however, we may find ourselves reaching a point where, perhaps only for a few moments, our thoughts become stilled, our inner chatter stops, and we seem to go down to the still point in our hearts, nearer to the place where God meets with us. When this happens, we are approaching what is sometimes called "pure prayer"—that is, in Dumitru Staniloae's words, "a total cessation of thought in the face of the divine mystery."[3] Most of us probably do not find ourselves in this state for long, but we may have moments when our prayer is truly wordless and we are not aware that it is going on. This may not happen easily or often. Such moments are gifts of God; we cannot bring them about, although by our inner silence we can prepare ourselves for them. They are not a necessary part of the prayer of silence, but may be one of its fruits, to be accepted with joy as part of our encounter with God.

During this life this encounter is always partial and incomplete, as we shall see; it is beyond our comprehension. It does not take place through our conscious, rational minds. It is an encounter of the feeling heart, not of the thinking mind. "When the mind has descended into the heart we no longer encounter God through ideas," says Staniloae. "Thinking about God interrupts direct encounter with him."[4] With our conscious minds we cannot fully comprehend this whispered exchange; nevertheless, we can be warmed and encouraged by the awareness that it is taking place. We can have a sense of a presence that we cannot fully grasp, of the reality of God dwelling within us that we cannot understand with our minds, of wonders that we cannot explain with our words. "If you seek the Lord in the depths," says Pseudo-Macarius, "there you will find him doing wonders."[5]

Two Wonders

God does his wonders within us in a number of ways. There are perhaps two special aspects of this encounter with God that are paradoxical, apparently contradictory, and full of wonder. The first is a sense of the greatness and otherness of God. This God who is present within us, in the secret heart of one small, insignificant, mortal person, is none other than the transcendent Other, the creator of heaven and earth, the ineffable one whom human words cannot describe, the unknowable one whose being human thought cannot grasp, the immortal, invisible, only wise God who dwells in light unapproachable or in deep and dazzling darkness. It is this God who mysteriously and wonderfully makes an abode within us and whom we can encounter in the depth of ourselves.

The word that comes to our lips when we are faced with the mystery and wonder of this presence is the word *holy*. This is a special word that is used in the Bible to speak of the otherness and separateness of God. Holiness is uniquely the characteristic of God—only God is holy. Anything else is "holy" only insofar as it belongs to or is connected with God. Our heart can be described as the "holy of holies" because it is the temple of the living God, the place where the Holy One makes himself present. When we reach down into our hearts and are given a sense of his presence, we are approaching holy ground. Here we inwardly put off the shoes from our feet, for the place on which we are standing is holy ground. Here we bow ourselves down in the presence of God's holiness. Here we sense that the Lord is in his holy temple and we must keep silent before him.

When we approach God in silent prayer, we do so with reverence, awe, and wonder, with a sense of who it is before whom we stand. Older writers spoke of this as the "fear of God," and they never tired of urging their readers to approach with fear and awe. "Beware," says Theophan, "lest in ceaselessly remembering God you forget also to kindle fear and awe, and the desire to fall down as dust before the face of God."[6] He adds elsewhere, "If someone should ask: how am I to pray? The answer is very simple: Fear God."[7]

To hold ourselves still in reverence before God in the prayer of silence is a form of adoration and praise. We can adore God in many ways, in hymns, in music, in the words of liturgy and poetry. But perhaps the deepest adoration is done in silence. When we are aware of the presence of God in his mystery and holiness, our natural response is to keep silent, and this is the purest form of praise. All praise, says Ephrem the Syrian, moves from sound to silence. The worship of heaven, he adds, is "the silent praise of angelic beings."[8] In the prayer of silence we approach God in reverence and awe, adoring the mystery of his being and the wonder of his presence in our hearts.

Along with this sense of the mysterious otherness of God goes something that seems to be its opposite: a sense that God is intimately close to us. This is the second wonder, and it is an extraordinary paradox. A whole world of difference lies between us and God. He is not a being like us, but is totally other. And yet, when we descend into our hearts, we have a strong and undeniable sense of his close, intimate, and personal presence within us. "Nothing is nearer to us than God," says John of Cronstadt. "He is the God of hearts, of the very hearts, and the heart, in its turn, is nearer than anything else to us."[9] In the depths of ourselves we find that there is a mysterious union between our hearts and God. God makes his home within us. He humbles himself, making himself small enough to enter our hearts. As in Christ "he emptied himself...and was born in human likeness" (Phil 2:7), so by an act of self-emptying or *kenōsis* he makes himself present in the depths of human hearts, and there we can encounter him.

That does not mean that there is no difference, or that God is to be identified with our hearts: he remains infinitely other. Nor does it mean that we can have a casual, cozy, or "chummy" relationship with God as with an equal. But neither does it mean that we are separate. Our hearts are united with God in a way that preserves the difference and does not annul the vast gulf of being. This sense of oneness and otherness, of closeness and separateness, of a God who is a part of us and yet infinitely beyond us, is an aspect of prayer in the depths that cannot be explained or even adequately described, but which is real in the experience of people of prayer. The God who is infinitely beyond us is so close to us that he seems to be a part of our very being. The one who is "greater than suns or stars" is also "closer than breathing."

In the previous chapter I spoke of the unique subjectivity of each of us. No one else can enter that deep place where I know myself to be Me and share my "Me-ness." There I am entirely alone, isolated from other human beings. But it is in that very place that I encounter God. Uniquely God shares my subjectivity; he is present in the place of my identity, knowing me as I know myself, sharing my sense of who I am. In my heart I am not seen by God from the outside as an object, nor do I experience God as an object. There is a togetherness, an intimacy that can be shared by no other human person. It is what we might call a union of shared subjectivity.

In life as we know it now, we experience this union in only a partial and incomplete way. We cannot now enter fully into union with God. But, as we shall see in a later chapter, the end of human life is the achievement of a union that is so close that it can be referred to as "deification"—a sharing in the nature of God. As we continue through the prayer of silence to reach deeper into our hearts and begin to encounter the twin wonders of the otherness and the closeness of God, we are given glimpses or a partial experience of that union, a foretaste of what is to come.

The Personal God

This encounter with God is possible because God is personal. That is not to say, of course, that he is a person, a kind of human being writ large. To call God a person would be to circumscribe him, to attribute to him the limitations of being an individual. But God is certainly not less than a person. He is not an impersonal force or some kind of absolute reality with no personal qualities. To say this would be to reduce God even further, to something less than human. The human person, the personal nature of a human being, represents the thing of highest value in all creation. God the Creator is, therefore, more than personal or, in the words of the Jewish philosopher Martin Buber, "supra-personal." We could perhaps call him the "absolute person," or the "infinite person." "God is a personal existence," says the theologian Christos Yannaras.[10] Therefore, the monk Silouan adds, "There is no other way for man to seek intercourse with the Divine than by personal prayer to a personal God."[11]

This means that in our prayer God is addressed and related to as "Thou" or "You." We approach him not as an object but as another subject. Because of the limitations of human thought and language we normally speak of God as an object, in the third person, as He (or She). But, properly speaking, God is always a subject, a personal reality, and our words about him are always spoken in his presence. Ideally, the pronoun we use for God should always be "You." Our relationship with God is never with an object but with this ever-present living subject, this You that confronts us as a person. Faith is a matter not of believing that there is a God, an objective reality whose existence we can debate, but of encountering another personal existence, infinitely greater than ourselves but a subject like ourselves. This is the only way we can know God. He is known not through the workings of our rational minds, nor through the use of our imagination—though both of these can help toward a deeper understanding of him—but through an I–Thou relationship in which we stand before him in the depth of our hearts and encounter him as a personal presence.

This personal I–Thou relationship is possible because we too are personal in nature. Being made in the image of God, human beings derive their personal nature from God the supreme or absolute person. We are persons because God is personal. In the words of Christos Yannaras, "Man has been endowed by God with the gift of being a person, with personhood, which is to exist in the same mode in which God exists."[12] By our very existence we share something of the personal nature of God, because God has made us that way. It is when we descend into our heart and stand before God that we truly know ourselves to be persons. Here in this secret place we are confronted with another who meets us on a person-to-person level. As we continue to be in his presence, we grow more fully into personal beings, able to relate to him in a deeper way. Because it is a relationship between personal beings, it is a reciprocal relationship. As we shall see in more detail in the next chapter, it is a two-sided relationship, characterized by freedom and sharing. Through it we become more free to be ourselves and also more able to relate to other people, not as objects but as fellow persons made like us in the image of God.

Limited

This holy yet personal God meets us in the depth of our heart, but, as was said earlier, in the course of this life this encounter is not complete: it is limited, hindered, and obscured. It is limited because of our human nature and the nature of God. Our encounter with God is not direct, as with another human being. In spite of God's closeness to us, paradoxically his presence is mysterious and elusive, and even at our times of deepest prayer we do not experience God as fully present. This is partly because of the very nature of God. He is infinite, his being is beyond us, mysterious and unknowable, so that even when he dwells in our hearts we cannot simply grasp him. Although our personal nature reflects his, and although we can have an intimate relationship with him, it remains true that his nature is totally different from the nature of a human being. In the words of Pseudo-Macarius, "This is God; the soul is not God. This is Lord; that is servant. This is Creator; that is creature. This is maker; that the thing made."[13] A vast and apparently unbridgeable gulf separates us mortal, time-bound creatures of earth from the infinite, immortal, eternal God. It is not given to us in this life to have a direct experience of God, face to face. We see him only "through a glass, darkly."

The limitation is due also to the fact that we ourselves cannot easily reach to the very bottom of our hearts, to the place deep within us where God is present. Our deepest self is largely hidden from us. It is true that there are mystics who are drawn deeper and deeper into their own hearts, and who can sometimes find that the door to that secret meeting place opens, and they are more directly aware of God. But for most of us the place where God dwells is a secret place into which we cannot normally penetrate, and it is within these mysterious and impenetrable depths of our hearts that God is present. In our silent prayer, however, as we descend deeper into our inner selves, we can become aware that somewhere within us, in a place we cannot reach, God is holding secret converse with our hearts even when we do not know it. There is a hidden dialogue between God and our inner selves, even if mostly we cannot hear it. When we engage in the prayer of silence we are listening in to this dialogue, eavesdropping at a door we cannot pry open, picking up the echoes and resonances of something we are unable to make out completely. There is a duet being played, but it is in the next room, and we can only partly hear the notes or get a sense of the tune.

Hindered

Our encounter with God is hindered also by the passions described in the previous chapter—the feelings, thoughts, and attitudes that arise out of our ingrained self-love and our inner fear. These have the effect of turning us in on ourselves and standing in the way of our relationship with God. To reach a deep relationship with God we have to do something to overcome these passions, or at least to reduce their influence over us. What can we do?

We can, of course, resist them. Once we have recognized the feelings and attitudes to which we are prone, we can make an effort to prevent them from taking us over. We can attempt to curb our envy and resentment and our desire to possess, or try to guard ourselves against the insidiousness of vainglory and pride. Orthodox writers, from the time of the Desert Fathers onward, attached a great deal of importance to "guarding the heart." Recalling the common biblical injunction to be alert and watchful (as in Mark 14:38; 1 Pet 5:6 and elsewhere), they urge the need to watch for and guard against evil thoughts entering the heart. But even when we do that we usually find that our passions continue to affect us. We may have some success in weakening them, but if we think we have got rid of them we frequently find that they return through the back door. Attempts to make ourselves into better, more moral, and less selfish people may yield some useful results, but the hidden fear and the secret self-love tend to remain, disguised perhaps by a generous and caring exterior. The struggle against the passions seems to be an unequal combat, a battle we cannot win.

It is only when we stand before God that we can realistically deal with our passions. Having descended into our heart and tried with honesty to recognize the feelings that are affecting them, the first thing to do is simply to call upon God for help. The early Fathers put great emphasis on the struggle against the passions, but they also knew that they could not win the battle by themselves. One of the Desert Fathers, Abba Macarius, was asked about the struggle. "There is no need at all," he said, "to make long discourses; it is enough to stretch out one's hands and say, 'Lord, as you will, and as you know, have mercy.' And if the conflict grows fiercer say, 'Lord, help!' He knows very well what we need and he shows us his mercy."[14]

But there are perhaps two more things we can do. The first is simply to acknowledge our passions before God. As we have seen, the passions are a part of the way we are internally, our inner state of being. In order to deal with them, we need to open this inner state to God and lay bare what we are really like within ourselves, acknowledging the particular passions to which we are prone. This can be painful, because it involves recognizing the gulf that exists between the person we believe God means us to be and the person we actually are. It also involves acknowledging that we are powerless to deal effectively with these passions and laying our helplessness before God. This is a form of confession and penitence. Confession, in the first place, is a matter not of listing the sins or wrong things we have done but of opening up our inner selves and our state of being before God. Penitence is not simply feeling remorse over things we should not have done but feeling the pain of acknowledging the passions that affect our inner state and therefore hinder our relationship with God. "The one who acknowledges his pain," said Isaac of Nineveh, "is close to healing."[15]

The second thing that goes along with acknowledging is offering. Having recognized something of the working of the passions within us, we can offer all of this to God. To offer is not simply to let go but to hand over, to ask God to take and accept what we are bringing. Our inner feelings, attitudes, and thoughts can all be offered to him. This is done as part of our total self-oblation, the complete offering of ourselves to God. We tend to think of offering God our good gifts, the best we have, so it may seem strange to offer him the negative things. But the offering of our whole self involves everything we have and are—the good and the bad—and our passions are a part of this. "Put upon [the altar] all your thoughts and your bad counsels," said Anthony of the Desert.[16] When we offer ourselves to God, we hand ourselves over to God just as we are, with all that is in us.

We can do this knowing that God accepts us just as we are. The gospel of Christ assures us that we do not need to overcome the passions by our own efforts before we are acceptable to God. When we acknowledge our inner state and offer it to God, he welcomes us to himself whatever we are like—which is another way of saying that God forgives those who are penitent. Moreover, by this process of acknowledging our helplessness and offering those things which we cannot get rid of by ourselves, we open the way for God to act. That is not to say that he simply removes our passions and perfects our relationship with him. But he uses our self-opening and self-offering to bring about a transformation within us. God works not through human power but through powerlessness, as was demonstrated most significantly in the death of Jesus on the cross. God's power works through human weakness, and so our very inability to get rid of our passions becomes an opportunity for him. The characteristic activity of God in relation to human beings is to bring good out of evil; even our passions, which are the product of evil within us, can be transformed and purified. "The Redeemer...when he comes," says Pseudo-Macarius, "transforms the thoughts of the soul and makes them divine, heavenly, good."[17] It is by the acknowledgment and offering of our pride that we learn humility. It is by the open confession of our inner fear that we learn to trust. It is by the transformation of our self-love that we learn to love God and other people. None of this happens at once: it is part of the slow process of God. But as we continue the practice of holding ourselves still before God in the prayer of silence, acknowledging our inner state in his secret presence and offering all to him, he can lessen the power of the destructive passions and gradually draw us into a closer relationship with himself.

Obscured

Our encounter with God is also obscured by a sense of God's absence. As we saw earlier, our human nature and the nature of God are such that God is never fully present for us in this life. He is always partially absent. This means that, alongside an awareness of his presence, we may frequently, or even constantly, have a sense of his absence. We do not encounter God face to face; we cannot grasp him or experience him directly with our physical senses. He is always in one way hidden, and his presence is at best elusive. So it is possible for some people to go all through life without recognizing or acknowledging God; and it is likely that for many people the sense of God's absence is more usual than an awareness of his presence. A sense of the absence of God is an inevitable accompaniment of our human life.

But there can be times when we are especially conscious of God's absence. Many people go through what are often called dry times, periods when the vitality and joy go out of their prayer and it becomes dull and laborious, times when praying seems tedious and they wonder if it is worthwhile. There are some—perhaps especially among people of deep prayer—who are confronted with a more acute sense of the absence of God. Sometimes God seems to withdraw and disappear completely. All attempts to reach him become useless, and prayer becomes meaningless. These can be times of deep darkness, without joy or hope, when there is nothing but emptiness and blackness. This may come about through some event in a person's life—bereavement, disappointment, or loss. But sometimes it happens without any obvious cause; God has hidden his face for no apparent reason.

People in that situation may find themselves able to do nothing more than repeat a daily office in a routine way; and for some even this can be impossible. There is no easy way out of this situation. It seems that all such a person can do is to wait in the darkness, holding on as far as possible to a belief that God is at work even in the blackness. Usually such times of darkness are followed in due course by times of sunshine, when the meeting with God becomes real again; and it is often possible, in retrospect, to recognize the hand and purpose of God even during the time when he had apparently withdrawn. But there are some very committed people of prayer who are cast into this pit of darkness for extremely long periods of time. It may even be that the bearing of this darkness and emptiness is a vocation to which a few people are called, a burden that is laid upon them for the sake of God's purpose in the world. There is a mystery here, before which we can only stand in awe.

It is important to realize that it is only people who know something of God's presence who are aware of and troubled by God's seeming absence. Those who have no sense of God and pay no heed to him are not concerned that he does not seem to be there. Indeed, it is often those who have penetrated most deeply into the prayer of silence who are most distressed when it seems that God has disappeared. It is not the godless but people of faith and prayer who find themselves crying out with the psalmist: "Why have you hidden your face from me?" This is because, in a strange way, what we experience as absence is in reality the reverse side of God's presence, the dark, hidden aspect of God's relationship with us. God's presence has been described as a brilliant and dazzling light, surrounded by a veil of darkness; and sometimes we are aware only of the darkness. But even in the darkness God has not totally withdrawn. Paradoxically, his absence is an aspect of a mysterious presence. It is only because of his presence that we know his absence.

This consciousness—that God is at best not fully present and at times seems to withdraw altogether—is an important part of the dynamic of the life of prayer, because it is out of this that our longing is born. When once we have sensed something of the presence of God, his absence produces a yearning for God, a deep desire to have him fully here, to be able to grasp him, to see him face to face. This can take different forms in different people. With some it may not be a conscious desire for God, but only a vague sense of dissatisfaction with even the best things of life and a feeling that there must be something deeper. Others may have a very conscious longing for closer contact with God, a deep desire to overcome the gulf between themselves and God and to commune directly with their Creator. Some people experience a feeling of acute yearning that continues throughout their life. The awareness of the absence of God can produce a thirst that cannot be quenched, a longing that will not be satisfied, an emptiness that cannot be filled, an ache that refuses to be comforted, a restlessness that lingers because here we do not fully find our rest in him. Whether it is something vague and undefined or something acute and compelling, it is this longing that is the engine of our prayer that impels us to go down deeper into our hearts and reach out in silence to God.

A Very Present Help

The encounter with God, then, is limited by our human nature, hindered by our passions, and obscured by God's seeming absence; but it does take place. His presence within us is real, and its effects upon us are positive. Through the prayer of silence most of us are given, in one way or another, a sense that God is indeed encountering us. As I said earlier, people's experience of this encounter varies considerably. Some have a very clear awareness of God at work within them, an experience of his presence in their hearts that is living and incontrovertible. For many of us, any such sense is fleeting—if it happens at all. We may occasionally be given what has been called a "flash of godhead," but our experience of God is usually something more indistinct. He meets us in the deep recesses of our heart, in a place which our thoughts cannot penetrate and our conscious minds cannot reach. The meeting takes place in secret, and we do not usually experience it fully or directly, but at one level of ourselves we do know it is going on. There is an encounter that is real even if we are only dimly aware of it. We have a sense that in the depth of our heart, in the secret place within us, God is indeed present.

In other words, we have a sense that God is "with us." This phrase, much used in the Bible, speaks not only of God's presence but also of his favor. It means that God is "for us"—another biblical phrase sometimes translated "on our side." God is not present in a disinterested way, unrelated to our well-being. His presence is a not a neutral but a positive thing; he is there to help us, to rescue us from the clutches of evil and to keep us safe. God is our helper, and it is simply by his being there, by the presence within us of one who is infinitely greater than us but closely united with us, that he helps us. In our distresses, our times of difficulty or emptiness and in the ordinary business of daily living, what we need more than anything else is for God to be with us. Even those who have no vivid experience of God and who may have been particularly aware of his apparent absence have found in times of deep darkness, when they are in the bleakest and loneliest place because of pain or loss, that they are not alone, that there is "something or someone" there in the depths of themselves, and that this presence, however faintly perceived, has brought comfort and hope.

This sense of presence can also make us aware of another thing of wonder: that the God who meets us also holds us. Through our encounter with God in the depths of silent prayer we can come to know in our hearts, and not simply with our heads, that no matter what may happen to us externally, our true inner self is being securely held. God's grasp of us is a fact, not something we hope for or strive after, but a given reality that we can be aware of as we engage in prayer. God holds our hearts, our inmost being, our true self, in his grasp. This means that he will keep us safe—not necessarily outwardly safe, protected from the hazards, misfortunes, and tragedies of life, but inwardly safe. Evil will continue to lay hold of us, but it will not wholly take us over, because God's hold on us will keep us from falling and we will not be lost. We can know that nothing can separate us from the love of God, nothing can snatch our inmost being out of his hands. This is a gift of the God who encounters us.

❖

The limpid heart is the dwelling place of divinity.

(Sahdona)[18]

It is not necessary to roam heaven and earth after God or to send our mind to seek him in different places. Purify your soul, O son of man...[and] you will be able to find him who is within you.

(Isaac of Nineveh)[19]

Let us, therefore, show awe when we sinners stand in the presence of this Majesty.... Let us, therefore, tremble at the magnitude of the sight of the Ineffable One.... And let us be filled with awe and trembling, falling on our faces in fear before him.

(Sahdona)[20]

We can't separate [God and ourselves] in our spiritual experience. We can't distinguish where one starts and the other stops. It is the experience of a union and interpenetration between God and ourself.

(Dumitru Staniloae)[21]

Made in the image of God, man is a personal being confronted with a personal God. God speaks to him as to a person, and man responds.

(Vladimir Lossky)[22]

Full of passions and weakness as we are, let us take heart, and let us in total confidence carry to Christ in our right hand and confess to him our helplessness and our fragility.

(John Climacus)[23]

If you are struggling against a passion do not lose heart, but surrender yourself to God, saying, "I cannot do this; help me, the wretched one."

(Abba Isaiah)[24]

In the beginning of the spiritual life the Holy Spirit gives people joy when He sees their hearts becoming pure.... He then departs and leaves them. This is a sign of His activity.

(Abba Ammonas)[25]

Prayer is the refuge of those who seek help, the source of salvation, the treasure-house of hope, the harbour from storms, the support of the weak, protection in temptations, the shield of deliverance in battle.

(Isaac of Nineveh)[26]

5

Mutual Relationship:
A Wonderful Exchange

God at Work

Prayer arises from a belief that God is actively at work and doing things. In the prayer of silence we open ourselves to this activity of God and make our response in return. To understand this, we need to give some thought to how God acts in the world. For this it will be useful to start with the Bible, which has been called the "book of the acts of God." From start to finish, the Bible is all about the activity or the works of God—what people of faith believed God had done, was doing, and was going to do. The Bible presents us with a "history of salvation," an overall account of God's plan and of how he went about it. It tells of how God created the world and filled it with good things; how he called a people to serve him, gave them a covenant and a law, chose kings to rule them, sent prophets to chasten and reprove them, and punished them with exile and then restored them; how he sent his Son to redeem the world and his Holy Spirit to lead, to guide, and to work in people's hearts; and how he worked through the apostles to spread the gospel. Of course, all of this involved human beings and required their response; but the story is essentially not about human deeds but about the activity of God.

If we follow the Bible we will believe that God is still active in the world of today and that, in our relationship with God, the most important thing is not what we do but what he does. The Christian life today is not so much a matter of our activity, of things we do for God, as a matter of our being open and responsive to the activity of God both within our hearts and in the world around us. The prayer of silence is one special way of holding ourselves open to this activity.

We should note, first of all, that prayer itself is an activity of God. We are accustomed to thinking of it as something we do, and of course there is some truth in this. It is we who decide to pray and decide what to pray about, and we who express the prayer in words or thoughts. But it is God who plants within us the desire to pray. It is God who draws us down into the place of prayer in our hearts. It is God who initiates in the secret place within us the dialogue that is the essence of prayer. By ourselves we can go through the motions of praying. But if prayer is more than the repetition of certain words or the expression of certain thoughts, if it is a contact and a converse with God himself and part of a relationship with him, it can only be done when he enables it and joins in converse with us. Prayer happens because God's Holy Spirit dwells within us. Left to ourselves, without the presence and help of the Spirit of God, we would not be able to reach out to God and pray. But when we go down into our inner selves, where our hearts are closely linked with God who dwells within us, our words and thoughts become not just the products of a human mind but a part of a dialogue with God. Our unspoken thoughts and the feelings we cannot express are turned into a deep form of prayer by the operation of the Spirit. As Paul says in the letter to the Romans, "The Spirit helps us in our weakness; for we do not know how to pray as we ought, but that very Spirit intercedes with sighs too deep for words" (Rom 8:26). Prayer, especially deep silent prayer, is the gift of God. "If you wish to pray," says Evagrius, "then it is God whom you need. He it is who gives prayer to the man who prays"[1]—words that have been picked up and repeated by other early spiritual writers. It can be said that when we reach a deep level of prayer it is God himself who prays within us. Our part is to be open to our own depths and to make room for the prayer of God.

According to the Bible, however, God is active in the world in other ways as well. If this is true, how do we know what he is doing? It is not obvious that he is at work either in the events that take place around us or in what is happening within us. It is often thought that an act of God is something out of the ordinary that has not come about through the normal processes of causation. If this is true, it would appear that he is not doing very much. Such acts of God do not happen very often. But the Bible offers us another way of looking at it. The actions of God reported in it were not obvious to the human eye. Although the biblical writers wrote of events that happened in the world, their main concern was not to offer us an ordinary account of historical events, nor to look for extraordinary happenings that occurred in the midst of them, but to discern the hand of God at work in and through these events. They saw the activity of God in all kinds of situations and in the most unlikely people: in a devious schemer like Jacob, in a foreign tyrant like Cyrus, and supremely in an unknown carpenter of Galilee. They looked at ordinary events brought about by the normal processes of causation and saw in them the working of God. It is this key aspect of the biblical writings that is especially important for the prayer of silence.

When we engage in silent prayer we do so in the belief that the God who dwells in our hearts is not static but is at work within us. The feelings and thoughts that arise within us are part of normal psychological processes, and we do not usually think of them as coming directly from God. But it is possible to believe that through what takes place within us in the normal way, God is at work, moving, stirring, nudging, comforting, admonishing, encouraging, calming, reassuring, challenging, and inspiring us. Similarly, external events that take place around us cannot usually be shown to have been brought about directly by God. We cannot prove or demonstrate that God is at work in the world, but we can believe that he is. When we pray in silence, we hold to this belief and open ourselves to what God is doing both in our hearts and in the life of the world about us.

What does it mean to be open to the activity of God? It means perhaps two things: first, trying to discern the hand of God in ordinary events. People who engage in prayer can have a sense of what God is doing within them and in the world. The eye of faith can see the hand of God in apparently ordinary things that happen, just as the writers of the Bible did. Discerning is not a matter of knowing for certain but of interpretation. What God gives to people who are steeped in prayer is not an unquestionable revelation of his actions nor a proof that he is at work, but a certain sensitivity to what we may call God's way of looking at things, which comes about through close communion with him. Through their relationship with God, people begin to have in them something of the mind that was in Christ Jesus (Phil 2:5), which enables them to interpret the events taking place around them, and the movements of thought and feeling within themselves, in the light of the activity of God. Prayer produces a way of looking at ordinary things, of seeing in them something more than chance events or the outcome of other people's intentions. "Those who persevere in prayer," says Pseudo-Macarius, "are taught secretly things they had not known before."[2] Discerning is a matter of seeing beyond the obvious aspect of events to what God may be doing through them.

Second, being open means saying yes to what God is doing—believing that God's work is going on within and around us—and holding ourselves ready to be a part of it. In the prayer of silence we make ourselves available to go along with the activity of God. We hoist our sail, as it were, to the wind of God's Spirit, so that we can be taken along by his movement. And we offer him our own expectations and plans, the things we are proposing to do, so that he can use them in what he is doing.

But even when we try to discern God's actions and to go along with them, we do not fully know what God is doing. God's activity, whether internal or external, is not verifiably demonstrated to us, and we may not be able to discern it even through our silent prayer. One of the characteristics of the actions of God is that they are usually done in secret. Just as the being of God is mysterious and unknown, so too are his actions. The Bible points to a God who in part reveals himself, but who also goes about things secretly. "Truly, you are a God who hides himself," says the book of Isaiah (Isa 45:15). One of the psalmists sees even the crossing of the Red Sea at the Exodus as a hidden act of God: "Your way was through the sea, your path through the mighty waters; yet your footprints were unseen" (Ps 77:19). Even in the person of Christ, God was not only revealed but also concealed—"veiled in flesh." Jesus was an ordinary man living in an obscure corner of the Roman Empire, in whom God was not obviously present. His life was a revealing of God only for those who had eyes to see; otherwise it was a hiding of God, a secret action discernible only by people of faith. Typically God works in secret.

This is partly because the main sphere of God's activity is the human heart. As we saw before, the heart is a secret place into which we cannot fully reach. Just as we cannot fully experience the presence of God within the depths of ourselves, so we cannot completely know what he is doing there. We may feel dissatisfied with this, because we have an urge to know; and we may be inclined to think that if we are unaware of God's activity he cannot be doing anything. But God does not always show us what he is doing, even in our own hearts. Nor can we fully discern his operations in the world outside us. Being open to the activity of God means in part being ready to accept this state of "not knowingness," to trust that God is working in a hidden way and to let ourselves be caught up in and carried along by this unseen divine action. Being willing to hold ourselves still in the darkness of not knowing what God is doing is part of the way of silent prayer.

A Reciprocal Relationship

The activity of God in the heart is not, however, one-sided: it forms part of what I have called God's reciprocal relationship with us. The Bible, as we have seen, insists that God is personal and has made us to be persons in his own image. His actions toward us are a part of a personal relationship with beings who reflect his own nature. Such a relationship, by its very nature, is reciprocal: there is a give-and-take in it, a to-ing and fro-ing. It is characteristic of the Bible that a number of words that are used in it to tell of God's activity in relation to us are used also of our activity in relation to God. The Bible tells, to give but a few examples, of God coming to us and our coming to God; of God holding us and our holding or clinging to God; and, mysteriously, of God blessing us and our blessing God. The Bible witnesses to the "wonderful exchange" between God and us. There is what Dumitru Staniloae calls a "simultaneous consciousness of our subject and of the supreme Subject, distinct from each other, but in relationship and reciprocal penetration."[3] The God who has given us a personal nature that mirrors his own then invites us into a relationship of mutuality, of give-and-take, in which we do for him what he does for us.

Perhaps the most significant element of this is the reciprocity or mutuality of love—God loves us and we love him. Indeed, this two-sidedness is built into the very meaning of the Old Testament word *hesed*, which is variously translated "loving-kindness," "mercy," "steadfast love" or simply "love." The Hebrew word refers to love in the context of a committed relationship, in particular, the relationship of the covenant between God and the people of Israel. The parties to the covenant were bound to one another by mutual *hesed*, "covenant love." The action of God in initiating the covenant and bestowing his love on his people was to be reciprocated by them. The reciprocal relationship arises out of mutual love—God's love for us and our love for God.

Although the relationship is mutual and reciprocal, an important aspect of it is that the initiative comes always from God: we do something for God because he does it for us first. This is emphasized in the Bible especially with respect to loving: "We love because he first loved us" (1 John 4:19); but it applies to other aspects of the "wonderful exchange" as well. Our ability to respond to God and give to him what he gives to us depends entirely on the prior action of God.

Seeking

There are perhaps three elements in this reciprocal relationship that deserve special attention because they are particularly important for the prayer of silence. The first of these is *seeking*. The verb "to seek" is a strong one. It means more than simply "to look for"; it implies desiring and wanting and involves intention, effort, and commitment. Seeking God in this way is an important theme in the Bible. The Old Testament prophets urge us to seek the Lord: "Seek the Lord while he may be found" (Isa 55:6); "Seek the Lord and live" (Amos 5:6). The psalmists recount that they are seeking him: "O God, you are my God, eagerly I seek you" (Ps 63:1); "In the day of my trouble I seek the Lord" (Ps 77:2). And Jesus himself said, "Seek first the kingdom of God and his righteousness" (Matt 6:33); "Seek, and you will find" (Matt 7:7). This refers not to a casual looking around for God but to a passionate desire to find him. Seeking God involves searching for him with one's "whole heart." The heart, as we have seen, means the deepest and most fundamental part of oneself, one's real, inner being; it is with this that we are to seek the Lord. And if we do, we will eventually find him. "When you seek me with all your heart, I will be found by you, says the Lord," according to the prophet Jeremiah (29:13). We cannot expect to find him if we seek only casually, occasionally, and with only a part of ourselves. But if we long for God and pour our longing into our seeking, if it is our heart's desire to find him, if we pursue our search for him with determination and an untiring resolve, then at the time and in the way of his choosing he will be found by us. To enter the prayer of silence is to seek God in this way. In the silence we reach out for him, gazing into the depths of ourselves, directing our thoughts and attention to him alone and seeking him with our whole heart.

But this is only one part of the seeking, and not the fundamental and most important part. For the truth is that not only do we seek God, but he seeks us. The seeking is reciprocal; and as in all aspects of this reciprocal relationship, it is God who takes the initiative. God seeks us before we seek him. Just as we love because he first loved us, so we seek because he has first sought us. The Bible tells of this mainly through the image of the shepherd. After developing the image to describe God's relationship with his people, the prophet Ezekiel announces, "For thus says the Lord God: 'Behold, I, I myself will search for my sheep, and will seek them out. As a shepherd seeks out his flock when some of his sheep have been scattered abroad, so will I seek out my sheep'" (Ezek 34:11–12). Jesus himself then takes up the theme in the well-known parable of the shepherd who left his ninety-nine other sheep to seek the one that was lost (Luke 15:3–7). The image is of God going out to look for his creatures. That we should seek God is not surprising: he is our maker, our life and our hope, and it is natural that we should seek him. But that he should seek us, wanting us for himself, desiring our presence, being dissatisfied until he finds us—that is truly a thing of wonder, which provides a powerful impetus toward prayer. In the prayer of silence we are impelled toward seeking God by the knowledge that long before we started consciously seeking him he was seeking us. We are drawn into a reciprocal relationship in which we seek each other. We seek, knowing that we will be found by the God who seeks for us.

Waiting

Because in our seeking we do not immediately find God, and because, as we have seen, God is never fully present for us in this life and at times may seem distressingly absent, we have to wait for him. *Waiting* is another element in our reciprocal relationship with God. Once again, this is a biblical theme. It is emphasized in a special way in the Psalms, where the phrase "Wait for the Lord" occurs frequently; and the theme is found also in the prophets and in the New Testament. To the biblical writers it was clear that God was not immediately present, nor could they expect him to act the very moment they called upon him. His presence and help could not be commanded but had to be awaited. Waiting for God was an important and inevitable part of the spiritual life.

In the modern Western world we tend to look on waiting in a very negative way. We dislike having to wait and sometimes take offense at being kept waiting. But waiting has always been seen as a positive and important aspect of silent prayer. In the deep inner silence, we wait for God. At times when the reality of God is particularly obscure, we may have to wait in darkness. In this silent waiting we are not actively doing anything, neither talking with God nor perhaps even enjoying his presence. We are indeed seeking him, but we do so not impatiently or restlessly but in a spirit of quiet, patient, and trustful waiting, because waiting is the mode of our seeking. It is not only a preliminary to prayer, something we have to do if we want to get deeper into prayer, a kind of necessary precondition to something greater. It is all that, but it is more than that: it is part of the prayer itself.

Waiting for God means waiting in hope. Sometimes this hope itself may be obscure, and we may not be sure what we are waiting for. But because we have at times been given some sense of his presence, we trust that God will act in his own time and way, and make himself known. We cannot control the actions of God: he acts in his own personal freedom, out of grace, not compulsion. As Theophan says, "As for what comes from grace...this we must simply await."[4] In the prayer of silence we wait in quiet expectation of his action and his presence. Waiting is a kind of invocation, a wordless calling upon God.

Even waiting, however, is reciprocal: we wait for God, and in an extraordinary way he also waits for us. This is expressed most clearly in one verse from Isaiah:

> *Therefore the Lord waits to be gracious to you;*
> *therefore he will rise up to show mercy to you.*
> *For the Lord is a God of justice;*
> *blessed are all those who wait for him.*
>
> (Isa 30:18)

The same thought is conveyed less directly elsewhere, especially in the prophets, where God is pictured as stretching out his hands all day long to a rebellious people (Isa 65:2; Rom 10:21), patiently hoping for a change of heart and waiting for his people to come to him. Even when they showed no sign of returning to him, God still waited.

When we wait for God in silent prayer, we know that before we began to wait for him, God himself was waiting for us. We wait because he first waited for us. So even when he seems distant or not available, we know with at least a part of our mind that somewhere in the shadows or the darkness God is waiting for us. The sense that even if I do not feel like praying God is actually waiting for me can provide a powerful incentive to pray. The knowledge that each is waiting for the other produces a kind of bond between us and God. This can be illustrated in a small way from ordinary human experience. Suppose, for example, that you are going by train to meet a friend. As you sit in the train waiting for it to arrive at the station, you know that your friend is waiting for you on the platform. The knowledge that you are both waiting gives pleasure, perhaps excitement, and is a kind of link or bond between you. So it is between us and God: the mutual waiting provides a bond that links us to him and encourages us to go on waiting. This is an important element in the prayer of silence. As Pseudo-Macarius says, "We ought soberly to have an attentive mind, waiting expectantly on God until he comes and visits the soul."[5]

Offering and Receiving

A third important part of the reciprocal relationship with God is *offering*. In our silent prayer we hand over our whole selves to him, all aspects of our life—our material and physical things, our plans and activities, our inner thoughts and feelings (including our "passions," as we saw earlier), and our hearts, the very center of ourselves, the place where I am uniquely Me. All of this is laid before God. This is an act of renunciation, of handing over, in which we ask God to take it all. We do this with confidence because we believe that it will be received. When we stretch out our hands to give ourselves to him, he stretches out his hands to receive. It is frequently emphasized that God is the Giver; but we need to remember that he is also the Receiver, that he takes and accepts us as we are, together with all that we bring to him, just as Jesus accepted the costly gift of the woman with the jar of ointment. It is in the confidence that the life we hand over to God will be accepted and will be safe in his hands that we quietly lay everything before him in silent prayer.

Unfortunately, however, this is not the end of the matter, because even when we do this with sincerity we usually find that, later on, in the course of ordinary living, we take back some of what we have offered, claiming some part of our life for ourselves again. In spite of our intentions at the time, our self-offering is not made once and for all: we constantly need to return and repeat it. Continuing day by day to lay ourselves before God and hand ourselves over to him is part of the pattern of silent prayer.

There is, however, another side to offering and receiving. Within the give-and-take of the mutual relationship, God also offers himself to us. This was, of course, done for us and demonstrated to us in a special way in Christ. At the incarnation, God was emptying himself in order to give himself to us; the death of Jesus on the cross was an act of self-offering that was God's way of reaching out to us. But it did not stop then: God continues to offer himself to us, to make himself available without stint or measure, in the mystery of the reciprocal relationship. The good things we are given day by day, externally through the world around us and internally within ourselves, are all a part of God's offering to us. The presence that, however elusively, is there for us when we wait for him is a gift offered to us.

Just as God receives what we offer to him, so it is for us to receive what he offers to us. Receiving, of course, is not the same as taking. When we receive a gift, we accept it and make it our own with thankfulness; to do this requires humility and openness. When we truly receive, we give back something to the giver. Christian people are frequently taught the importance of giving: "It is more blessed," we are reminded, "to give than to receive." But there is a grace of receiving as well as of giving, a grace that adorns a truly Christian life. Being willing to receive is in a special way a part of silent prayer, for when we make ourselves still before God we are holding out our hands to receive, opening ourselves to the gifts he is giving us now, and to the unknown gifts we will be offered in the hours and days ahead.

So there is a reciprocity of offering and receiving: God offers and we receive; we offer and God receives, in a deep mutual sharing. By the humility of our receiving we enable God's giving. By his humble acceptance of our offering God enables our giving. In this, as in every other aspect of this reciprocal relationship, the action of God comes first. It is because God is a giving and receiving God that we can be giving and receiving people. The reciprocity is expressed and enacted in a special way in the sacrament of the Eucharist. In it the gifts we offer as symbols of our selves and our life are received by God and turned into the means by which he offers to us his life, which we in turn receive and take to ourselves. The Eucharist is an expression of the "wonderful exchange" that is at the heart of the Christian life and that starts with God's offering of himself to us in Christ. In the prayer of silence we enter more fully into this exchange. As we lay ourselves open before God in stillness, we allow a reciprocal relationship to grow in which each seeks and waits for the other and each offers to and receives from the other within the mystery of a personal relationship with God.

Sharing in God's Nature

One further point deserves mention, even though it takes us beyond the subject of silent prayer. This reciprocal relationship is part of a process that leads on to an even more remarkable relationship. The process started with God's creation of human beings in his own image. We were made to be like God, to mirror and reflect his own personal nature and to be able to respond to him. Being made in God's image, we can then enter the kind of reciprocal relationship that we have been discussing here. In our holding on to God, seeking him, waiting for him, offering to him, receiving from him, knowing, blessing, and loving him, we respond to the God who first does all these things for us. Through this mutual partnership of intimate give-and-take we become more and more closely bound to God and he to us. But this itself is still only a stage in the process: it leads on to a further stage in which we are finally united with God. The end and purpose of the process, and of life itself, are what is sometimes called "deification" or "becoming divine" (*theōsis* in Greek), a sharing in the very nature of God.

This is an aspect of spiritual theology that has been especially emphasized by Orthodox writers, ancient and recent. It is based on New Testament teaching expressed, for example, in the words of Jesus' prayer in John 17:22–23: "That they may be one as we are one; I in them and you in me"; or in the teaching of Paul and John that we are to become children of God (Rom 8:15–17; Gal 4:5–7; John 1:12); or in the saying in 2 Peter 1:4 that God gave us his promises so that we "may become participants in the divine nature." According to this teaching, to be a child of God, to be one with him and to share in his nature, is the purpose of human life; and to enable this to happen was the purpose of God's assumption of human nature in Christ. This is emphasized in the classic statement of the great fourth-century writer Irenaeus of Lyons, which has been repeated and expanded by others throughout the years: "God became man in order that man might become god."[6] As we shall see later on, this deification is the culmination of a process by which, having been made to reflect God's personal nature, we then develop a reciprocal relationship with him, and this in turn blossoms out into a fuller relationship of union, in which we share in the being of God without ceasing to be ourselves. In the words of Maximus the Confessor, "The deified person, while remaining completely human in nature...becomes wholly God."[7] This is not something external but something that happens inwardly and mysteriously: a uniting of our deepest self, our heart, with the being of God; a coming home to share in the life of the Being who gave us life. This does not happen yet: it is still to come, in a life we do not yet know. But if by our silent prayer we begin to take part in the "wonderful exchange" between us and God, we can perhaps become aware, however dimly, that there is another stage; that the mutual relationship of sharing that we now know is the precursor of a deeper relationship in which we will be drawn into the very being of God, to be immersed and enfolded in him; and that this will be the fulfillment of our being.

You cannot discover from the teaching of others the beauty of prayer. Prayer has its own special teacher in God, who "teaches man knowledge." He grants the prayer of him who prays.

(John Climacus)[8]

Spiritual knowledge is perception of the hidden.

(Isaac of Nineveh)[9]

The presence [of God] is already in [people], in their "heart," in that most central of centers, that deepest of depths, which is also open to transcendence.... But this presence in the heart is unconscious.

(Olivier Clément)[10]

God offers himself, wishes to disclose himself, but he does not force us. His power is the power of love, and love wants the freedom of the beloved. God speaks, and at the same time keeps silence; he knocks at the door and waits.

(Olivier Clément)[11]

Let us then seek him out, let us endeavor to attain to him, that we may lay hold of him.

(Symeon the New Theologian)[12]

Strive to please the Lord, always waiting expectantly for him from within, seeking him in your thoughts.... For when he first sees you seeking after him, and how you are totally waiting expectantly without ceasing for him, he then teaches and gives you true prayer.

(Pseudo-Macarius)[13]

The human being is an animal who has received the vocation to become God.

(Basil of Caesarea)[14]

Deification is God's perfect and full penetration of man.
(Dumitru Staniloae)[15]

What must be deified in us is our entire nature belonging to our person which must enter into union with God.
(Vladimir Lossky)[16]

6

Prayer and the World: A Partnership

To be in a reciprocal relationship with an active God is to have a share in what he is doing or, in other words, to cooperate with him. How does this happen? In this chapter I mean to look at two important ways in which we can share in the work of God by means of the prayer of silence.

Doing God's Will

One way of cooperating is by trying to do God's will, to do the things God wants us to do. Doing the will of God is an important theme in the New Testament, found both in the Gospels and the Epistles. Jesus himself said that it was only those who did the will of his Father who would enter the kingdom of heaven (Matt 7:21). But how do we know what God's will is? From the Bible and from the teaching of Jesus we can have a general understanding of what kind of world God wants to bring about and of how he wishes us to live; but how do we discover what he wants us to do at any particular time, or what decisions we should make about our future? The answer would seem to lie in a kind of prayer in which we listen to God.

But praying to God in order to ascertain his will for us raises some questions and difficulties. Does listening mean that in our prayer we expect God to speak to us and tell us what he wants us to do? Some people find that this does indeed seem to happen from time to time. During a period of prayer, or as a result of it, they find themselves with a clear sense that God is directing or calling them to do something. Such a sense is not to be ignored; it requires attention and thought. It may come from God and provide a pointer to the direction a person should take; but it may equally be an illusion. It is all too easy to conclude that God is speaking to us, when what we are hearing simply arises from our own psychological processes, from the projection of our own wishes onto God. The dangers of self-deception are real. The early Fathers believed that the demons tried to deceive them by setting before them a way that seemed to be the way of God but which in fact drew them away from him. Russian Orthodox writers speak of the dangers of *prelest,* or "illusion." "To be in prelest is to be in a state of beguilement and illusion, accepting a delusion as reality."[1] "Illusion," says Theophan, "comes as a charmer who seeks acceptance by man, and from his acceptance gains power over him."[2] Our own inner voices can persuade us that what we ourselves want is the will of God, or conversely, that the hard or difficult way must be what God wants, just because it is hard!

Then there is a difficulty of an opposite kind. Some people find themselves frustrated because, although they want to do God's will and try to listen to him in prayer, they are given no clear sense of what God wants. This can be very puzzling. If God wants us to do something, why doesn't he tell us? Sometimes people conclude that the fault must be theirs. Perhaps they have not prayed hard enough; or God won't speak to them because they have done something wrong. Some people even find themselves adopting, perhaps without realizing it, what amounts to a very extraordinary view of God and his dealings with people: apparently he has something he wants them to do, but he refuses to tell them what it is, leaving them to find out for themselves and then blaming them if they don't get it right! Rather than entertaining such an idea it is better to recognize that God does not normally communicate by speaking to us directly in this way. Rather than castigating ourselves for not hearing his voice, we should perhaps recognize that this is not his method of communication.

So how can our prayer enable us to do what God wants? Perhaps we need to think of God's will differently and to engage in prayer in a different way. While God undoubtedly has a will and a purpose for humankind, he does not necessarily have a worked-out scheme, or a predetermined plan, about what each of us should be doing to cooperate with him. God the supreme Person relates to us as persons, drawing us into a reciprocal relationship of give-and-take and of personal freedom, in which both we and God offer to the other and receive from the other. It is not a matter of his having a fixed will for us that we have to obey, but of our attempting, by our own free will and in the best way we can, to further the objectives we share with God within our mutual relationship. Doing the will of God is not simply a matter of conforming to his wishes. God gives us free personal choice about how, in the course of our ordinary life, we attempt to cooperate with him and promote his purposes. Even when it comes to deciding important questions about our future, God does not simply expect us to do what he wants; doing God's will still leaves us with our own free choice. This is not to say that he abandons us to our own devices. Our thinking and decision making about what we should do are carried out within a relationship in which God is with us. When we do this, as someone has said, it is as if God were saying, "You choose, and I'll be with you."

Probably most of us do not experience God "speaking" to us directly. His communication with us is principally through our hearts, and, as we have seen, the heart is a secret place, whose ultimate depths we cannot reach. It is here that God speaks with us in a dialogue that we do not completely hear. We may not know with our conscious minds what it is that God is saying to us, or where he is taking us. God works his will in us not principally through messages to our minds but through the feelings, intentions, and motives that determine our actions and our life in the world. It is true that these actions, as we have seen, are often governed by our passions, the feelings that arise from the self-love and fear that are always present within us and may lead us astray. But that is not the whole of it; for God is also present within us, drawing these inner feelings toward himself and in this way affecting and influencing our actions, turning them in the direction of his will. When this happens, his will is done within us largely without our knowing it. That is not to say that we never make conscious decisions to do what we believe to be in keeping with God's will. We constantly have to decide how to act, and when we are faced with difficult choices, we need to use our minds and our best judgment to decide as wisely as we can. But doing the will of God is less a matter of our conscious minds than of our secret hearts. It is a question not of reaching the correct decision in the light of what God wants but of opening ourselves to what God is doing within us.

Sometimes it is right simply to follow our "heart's desire"—our basic inner wish, the thing we want to do more than anything else, the most profound urge within us. What this is may be partly hidden from us, tucked away in the background and not easily recognized. It may not apparently have anything directly to do with God. Our secret desire may have to do with how we would like to spend our time or develop our life. Perhaps this may be simply a selfish wish that may be dismissed as such. But if through our silent prayer we have a deep reciprocal relationship with God, if by seeking, waiting, offering, and in other ways we are engaged in this wonderful exchange, then he will do his work within our hearts, affecting and moving them and drawing them to himself. In this way our heart's desire will be molded and shaped by the secret influence of the Holy Spirit into conformity with the mind of God and will bear the stamp of our relationship with him. In these circumstances our heart's desire may be a pointer to the will of God, so that it is sometimes right and good to search for it and then to yield to and follow it in the confidence that it is born of God.

Another way of putting this is to say that doing the will of God arises naturally out of love. We have seen that love is the basis of our mutual relationship with God—his love for us and ours for him. In this situation our decisions are made on the basis not of rules or commands but of mutual love. They are the natural and perhaps unconscious overflow of our love for God. Just as in a close human relationship two people cooperate not by rules or by deliberate negotiation but by a natural coming together of desire and thought as a result of love, so it is in our relationship with God. Our decisions and actions arise from a togetherness in love, as part of our mutual exchange with God.

What, then, has this to tell us about prayer and listening to God? Listening is not a matter of trying to hear a message from God to tell us what to do. To do that is to deny the freedom of the interpersonal relationship. But there is another kind of listening, a kind of deep, inner listening. As we saw in chapter 1, there is a way of listening not to the sounds that are coming to us but to silence—the silence around us and within us and the silence of God. By listening to our own inner silence we open ourselves to what God is doing within us and to where he is leading us. We listen not to hear the voice of God addressing his commands to our conscious minds but to let ourselves be influenced by his unspoken promptings, the voiceless stirrings of his Spirit within our hearts. We attune our ears to the silence of God, because it is through this silence that he communicates with the silence deep within us.

In the context of the prayer of silence, then, doing the will of God takes on a different aspect. Instead of trying to discover what God wants and then setting out to do it, we open ourselves to an inner relationship of mutual self-offering, in which our hearts are moved by his silent workings within us, our wills are increasingly merged with his in love, and our decisions and actions tend more and more to be prompted by our togetherness with him.

Intercession

The kind of prayer in which we pray for other people about whom we are concerned, and for situations of need in the world around us, is another way of cooperating with God. In the prayer of intercession, whether done privately or corporately with other people, we remember before God people whom we love, people who are sick or suffering, places in the world where there is trouble or need, and any situation that is giving us special concern. Prayer of this kind comes naturally to us—even those who do not usually go in for prayer will call on God to help if they are acutely concerned about someone they love. We have a deep sense that we are doing good for people by praying for them. Intercession is an expression of our faith in God and our love for other people, and it is an important part of prayer.

But intercessory prayer raises a number of questions that have no easy answer: Does it have any effect? As a result of our prayers does God intervene to change the course of things in the world or the lives of other people? Do our prayers persuade God to do something he would not otherwise be doing? Is it right to pray for outcomes that we would like but that may not be the will of God? Should we make specific and detailed requests to God about other people and their needs, or should we confine ourselves to broad general petitions and intentions?

We will never find complete answers to all our rational questions, because prayer is not entirely a rationally comprehensible business. Nevertheless, some of the difficulties about intercessory prayer disappear when we think of it in a different way. It is helpful to see intercession not so much as making requests of God or asking him to do things, but as a way of cooperating with him. If we recognize that God is active in his world to further his purpose, prayer is a way of sharing in this activity. It is a matter not of trying to persuade him to do something he would not otherwise have done but of aligning ourselves with and supporting what he is doing anyway. It is a matter not primarily of asking God to do what we want but of offering him our concerns, our care for other people, our anxieties about the state of the world, and asking him to use this to further his work. It is something that flows naturally from our reciprocal relationship with God.

That is not to say that we will never express our own wishes and desires. Of course, when we long for peace in the world, for the end of famine and hunger, or for someone we love to recover from a serious illness, we will pour out this longing to God. But we will present this as what it is, our wishes, our desires, and the way we ourselves would like to see things happen—desires and wishes limited by our restricted understanding and to some degree warped by our selfish passions—and we will ask God to accept these as expressions of our feelings and our concern and to use them in his way. Indeed, it is important that our prayers of intercession should contain our feelings. Praying for other people is not a mechanical act of repeating names but the offering of our concern, allowing the feelings we have about other people and the world to be placed before God, so that he can transform them and incorporate them in his purposes. In this way our intercessions become part of the exchange of prayer.

This suggests that, while our prayers for others are normally expressed in thoughts and words, the essence of intercession lies deeper and is related to the prayer of silence. Borrowing a phrase from the late Archbishop Michael Ramsey, we may describe intercession as "being with God with others on our heart." Having others on our heart means feeling for them, caring about them, having a continuing concern for them, not in a superficial way but deeply within ourselves, in our heart. It means in some small measure taking their woes upon ourselves, in mind and imagination bearing a little of what is happening to them. As one of the early Egyptian Fathers, Mark the Ascetic, explained: "Every man has to bear what befalls not only for himself but also for his neighbor, inasmuch as he has taken him upon himself."[3] To have others on our heart is to take what befalls them upon ourselves. This is a difficult and costly thing to do, and most of us do it only in a very limited way; but it is an aspect of true intercession. With this heart-felt concern we then simply place ourselves before God, taking some time to "be with" him. To intercede is not essentially to make a petition or to name names or list our concerns. It is to stand in the presence of God for the sake of someone else, opening our hearts and all that is in them as we wait before him in silent prayer.

To pray in this way is to keep a kind of vigil, to "keep watch with Christ" in the face of the world's troubles, to take part in a perpetual silent vigil being observed by people who stand together before God for the sake of the world. When we engage in this silent intercession we are not alone but are linked with thousands of others who are doing the same. Even at times when we are not consciously praying, we can know ourselves to be part of this worldwide community. From time to time, by day or by night, we can deliberately take our place alongside them, joining in this silent vigil.

In the prayer of silence we are content to recognize that our prayer is not powerful in the world. As we hold ourselves before God for the sake of the world and other people, we do not wield power to influence events or change what is happening. That is not to say that intercessory prayer is ineffective; it is effective when, by standing before God in our powerlessness, we become channels in a small way for the mysterious work of the God who works by powerlessness.

But there are other and deeper aspects of intercession. We are all aware of terrible events that take place in the world, and so it is natural and right that we should pray for those who suffer as a result of them. But if we remember Jesus' prayer for those who crucified him, we will pray also for those who commit these terrible deeds. This is a type of intercession that is very specially Christian and to which all Christian people are called. In our prayers of intercession we remember evildoers, and we call upon God, in the words of the Lord's Prayer, to "deliver us from evil," to rescue both us and the people of the world from the hidden power of evil and from its effects.

And we can go a step further. We can recognize that evil deeds are the result of human passions—emotions, attitudes, and motives situated deep within the human heart—and that these passions are found not only in a few wicked evildoers but in everyone. Through our passions we all have a share in the broken and troubled state of the world and are part of the chaos of the world. In the light of this there is a special kind of intercession to which some people—perhaps only a few—are called. In this kind of prayer we not only place ourselves silently before God; we also place ourselves in mind alongside people who are caught up in evil. Being aware that we ourselves have a share in the world's evil, and acknowledging that we too are subject to the same passions and are caught up in a less obvious way in the same web of evil, we number ourselves among them. In this way we bring our own little bit of the world's disorder and place it before God. We allow ourselves to be stretched between the evil of the world from which we cannot escape and the mercy of God who cares and suffers for his world; and we look for his mercy to deliver everyone, the "good" and the "bad" alike. By doing this we share, to a very small degree, in the work of Christ, who was made "to be sin who knew no sin" (2 Cor 5:21), who was "numbered with the transgressors" (Isa 53:12), and who bore the desolation of the cross.

There are some who have done this in an especially deep and costly way. Silouan, a monk of Mount Athos in Greece, was one who felt a special vocation to an inner solidarity with the world's evil and its consequences while holding on to faith in God. He tells how, during a period of prayer, the words came to him: "Keep your mind in hell and despair not."[4] He felt that, for the sake of people in the world, he had to bear the darkness and torment of separation from God that is the result of evil, without becoming a victim of despair. This is an extreme example, beyond the experience of most of us, but it illustrates a particular approach to intercession for the world's evil. It is likely that even among those who engage in the prayer of silence there will not be many who are drawn to this kind of prayer. But for those who are, it can become a profoundly Christlike form of intercession.

In a less unusual way, this approach can find expression through the practice of the prayer of silence. Some forms of rhythm prayer that are used in silent prayer, such as the Jesus Prayer and an alternative form that I suggested in chapter 2, include the words "Have mercy on me." This may seem to be exclusively focused on *me* as an individual, as if I were only concerned to receive God's mercy for myself. But if I recognize that I have a share in the disorder of the world, this prayer becomes a plea for God's mercy not on myself in isolation but on my little bit of the broken humanity of which I am part. If I am concerned with the evil of the world, I cannot pray about it as if it were simply something "out there" involving other people alone: I need to start with myself and lay my own part of it before God. I am part of a whole, and in praying for God's mercy on myself I am praying also for the whole. The words "Have mercy on me," repeated in our inner silence and said in solidarity with the world and its needs, thus become a real and vital form of intercession.

This in turn has implications for other aspects of life. We can place ourselves alongside other people in prayer only if we do the same in our attitudes to them day by day. Insofar as we secretly regard ourselves as superior to or better than others, we cannot sincerely stand beside them in prayer. If we inwardly condemn their faults or point a finger at their failings, we cannot be alongside them in our common involvement in the world's evil. That is one reason why the early Fathers placed great emphasis on the Lord's command not to judge others (Matt 7:1). In judging or condemning others we condemn ourselves, since we are in the same position and, like them, require God's mercy. Indeed, the Fathers of the desert made a deliberate effort not to notice others' misdeeds and even to hide or "cover" them so that they would not be seen by others. They believed that God himself not only exposes our sins but also, by bearing and forgiving them, covers them over and blots them out. It was said of one of the greatest of them that "just as God protects the world, so Abba Macarius would cover the faults which he saw, as though he did not see them; and those which he heard, as though he did not hear them."[5] In the prayer of silence, we seek to cover the wrongs of others as we pray that God in his mercy will cover ours. In this way it is possible even for us to have a very small share in the work of Christ and to cooperate in the activity of God.

Seen in this way, intercession is more than prayer in a narrow sense. It can, of course, be a basic and easy form of prayer, a simple call to God to help someone in need. But it can also be a mysterious, profound, and costly thing, involving an attitude to ourselves and to other people, and a stance before God that finds expression not only in our prayer but in our life. In the context of the prayer of silence, it can become a way of being, an offering not only of our concerns for other people but also of ourselves, to be used by God as part of the wonderful exchange.

❖

Those who practice obedience develop Christian compassion for the torment of all humanity, and their prayers take on a cosmic dimension.... This sort of prayer makes man aware of his unity with all mankind.... Such prayer effectively furthers the salvation of the world, and every Christian must sooner or later come to pray for the whole world.

(The Monk Silouan)[6]

Rebuke no one, revile no one, not even men who live very wickedly. Spread your cloak over the man who is falling and cover him. And if you cannot take upon yourself his sins and receive his chastisement in his stead, then at least patiently suffer his shame and do not disgrace him.

(Isaac of Nineveh)[7]

At the very moment when we hide our brother's fault, God hides our own, and at the moment when we reveal our brother's fault, God reveals ours too.

(Abba Poemen)[8]

To pass judgment on another is to usurp shamelessly a prerogative of God, and to condemn is to ruin one's soul.

(John Climacus)[9]

7

Prayer and Life:
A Process

In the foregoing chapters we have explored the topic of silent prayer, as it were from the inside, looking at what takes place between us and God in the depths of our hearts. But the prayer of silence also has practical aspects, implications for the way we live. In this final chapter we will look at some of these.

Our Work and God's Grace

Silent prayer is not easy. Just to be quiet with God may sound simple, as if it were a kind of spiritual relaxation that makes us feel better. But, in fact, if we take the prayer of silence seriously, we find that it is hard work and requires us to exert ourselves in a number of ways. Of course, it isn't all hard work. Prayer is also letting go, abandoning oneself into the hand of God, letting oneself be held, and enjoying a sense of his presence. But, as we have seen already, the act of praying itself requires concentration, and often this does not come to us easily. We are often beset by distractions and led astray by the subtle operation of our passions. The task of keeping our mind in our heart and our attention focused on God is difficult and not always immediately enjoyable. In addition, it is sometimes hard to find the time needed for silent prayer and to avoid interruptions. It is often tempting to skip our times of prayer, perhaps on the very understandable grounds that we must not be too rigid or rule-bound in our practice. We can also be discouraged by what seems to be lack of results or progress and by the apparent absence of God; and from time to time we may be tempted to give up prayer altogether as not worth the effort. It also requires, as we shall see, a degree of inner detachment from the things of the world, a willingness to give up our desire to possess and control and to renounce our own plans and expectations.

Because of this, continuing with the prayer of silence requires commitment, perseverance, and a determination to go on with it even at those times when it may seem pointless. We cannot expect to engage meaningfully in silent prayer unless we are prepared to work at it diligently. But, paradoxically, that does not mean that our efforts bring success. The close mutual relationship with God does not come about by what we do. Everything that emerges from a life of prayer comes from God and through his initiative. Even our determination and commitment are possible only because of God. Our effort arises from and goes hand in hand with the grace or gift of God, who plants within us the desire to pray. If it is God who lays upon us the demand of prayer, it is also God who gives us the power to do it. In a way that we cannot fully understand or explain, God gives what he demands; with him the demand and the gift are one. This paradox is well expressed by Theophan: "You will achieve nothing by your own efforts alone; yet God will not give you anything unless you work with all your strength."[1]

That is not to say that our endeavors are a precondition of God's grace or that we have to earn God's grace by first making an effort ourselves. Grace is God's free gift—God giving himself to us without condition or price. All we need to do is open our hands and our hearts to receive it. Grace, indeed, evokes our receptivity and draws forth from us the corresponding grace to accept God's gift. But it also inspires us to exert ourselves in prayer. Within the relationship of exchange between us and God, his grace and our endeavors come together and are rolled into one. God's grace calls forth our effort, and our effort invites his grace. This is yet another aspect of the mutual or reciprocal character of the inner life of prayer: we and God respond to one another within the give-and-take of the relationship. But as with every other aspect of this exchange, God's part comes first. We make the effort to reach out to him in prayer because he first reaches out to us with his grace and help.

Life in the World

Most of us who attempt to practice the prayer of silence have to do so while living ordinary lives in the world. This has its own difficulties and challenges, as well as its satisfactions. From much of what is written about silent prayer, however, one might conclude that to engage in it seriously one needs to live the monastic life, totally devoted to the life of prayer. This impression arises partly from the fact that a great deal of what has been written about prayer, especially in the early centuries, was written by monks for monks. Important spiritual writers of the Orthodox tradition such as Evagrius, John Climacus, and Isaac of Nineveh wrote for their fellow monks or even for solitaries, and some parts of their teaching and advice on prayer cannot easily be applied to the life of those who live in "the world." This does not mean, however, that the prayer of silence is only for monastics and hermits or needs to be done in isolation from the rest of life. On the contrary, it is important that many people should be able to develop what has been called a "mixed life," a way of living in which the prayer of silence plays an important part, while they continue to live in the ordinary world and take part in the life of society.

If the prayer of silence is to be a meaningful part of our lives and to have some of the features I have been trying to describe in these chapters, it needs to be supported by and integrated with a way of life that does not conflict with it, provide unnecessary distractions from it, or put hindrances or encumbrances in our way. We need a way of living that is based on the same aims and priorities as we have in our times of prayer. Such a life will be characterized by a measure of simplicity and detachment. This does not mean that we will live in poverty, without possessing anything. So long as we live in the world and are part of human society we need some possessions, and in a spirit of thankfulness we will accept, use, and enjoy them. But it does mean that we will try not to be attached to them or excessively anxious about them, and that we will not set our hearts on increasing them. We will aim to live in a fairly simple way, so that we are not too much encumbered by this world's goods, nor distracted from prayer by having to pay too much attention to them. Our aim will be to free our minds from having to give a lot of thought to possessions, and to free our hearts from emotional attachment to them, so that we can focus on God and the work of prayer without hindrance. We need to withdraw from the world while remaining in it; to live in it and take part in its life but be detached from it; to be in it but not of it. To quote Theophan again, "Anyone seeking the Lord must withdraw from the world, from everything passionate, vain or sinful....

To withdraw from the world does not mean to run away from family life or society, but to give up whatever customs, rules, habits or claims go against the spirit of Christ which is growing within us."[2]

This kind of detachment is essentially an inner thing. It means sitting lightly to material possessions and inwardly letting go of the desire to acquire more for ourselves. It involves allowing ourselves to be stripped of the mental stratagems and emotional attachments that we use to prop ourselves up and that prevent us from trusting God completely and abandoning ourselves to him. This inner stripping does not happen easily or quickly. To make it possible we need to have a certain discipline of life. What form this should take is something most of us have to decide for ourselves. Those who live as ordinary people in the world are not provided with an ordered pattern of religious life and a routine of offices and periods of prayer, as in a monastic house. We may be committed to living under a personal "rule," either one given to us or one of our own devising, but we still have to apply it in such a way that it fits in with the necessary demands of living in the world.

To live a "mixed life" of this kind we need to try to get the balance right, to find time and opportunity both for prayer and for "worldly" activity. This means giving serious thought to our priorities and perhaps giving up or cutting down on some activities that are good and important in themselves but do not allow the time and mental space needed for developing the prayer of silence. But living a life of prayer in the world does not mean regarding prayer as the only important thing and the rest of life as secondary: it means seeing our active life in the world as equally a part of our Christian vocation alongside our prayer. In the mixed life the two go together: the active life informs prayer, and prayer supports the active life. It is not always easy to achieve the proper balance, and there is no ready-made formula for doing so. We need to work it out for ourselves in the light of our circumstances, and different people will approach it in different ways.

There is, however, one quality that will generally characterize a life of silent prayer lived in the world: it will be largely hidden. The mutual relationship with God that grows up through the prayer of silence is, by its very nature, not shown and made public to all. The prayer that occurs in the secret place of our hearts does not have a demonstrable impact on life around us. It cannot be seen to be powerful or effective. This means that people who engage in this kind of prayer must be content to be powerless, to live without dominating other people, manipulating them to do what we want, or subtly imposing our will on them. Our relationships with others will be based on the hidden life of prayer in which we are brought into relationship with the God who works secretly and without visible power.

This hiddenness does not mean, however, that those who engage in the prayer of silence are of no use or value to the world. This kind of prayer, as we have seen, is a way of cooperating with God and allowing his work to be done in and through us. There is perhaps no more important thing to be done for the sake of the world than to hold its life before God in silent offering. Those who do so are helping to shield the life of the world from chaos and evil. Olivier Clément speaks of them as people "whose prayer defends and protects the world, saves it from falling apart, and becomes the life-blood of truly creative undertakings."[3] This is done in a special way by members of religious communities living the monastic life, but those who undertake this work of prayer while living in society are also important for the life of the world. By binding themselves into a relationship with God while standing firmly in the world, they form a bridge for the caring, challenging, transforming, and healing grace of God to enter the lives of people. The task of holding these two aspects of life together in a "mixed life" is demanding and difficult, but it is one that is vital for the life of the world today. There is a great and urgent need for men and women who will see this as their vocation and commit themselves to it.

A Long Process

Finally, we should recognize that the prayer of silence is part of a long process. When we engage in it, we have to be prepared for the long haul. We do not immediately see results or find that the world or our lives have dramatically changed. Certainly, it produces a deepening of our relationship with God in a way that brings comfort, reassurance, and hope, and gives meaning to life. As we continue in it we may at times find ourselves able to touch, as it were, the hem of his garment, to catch a glimpse of his holiness, to sense the wonder of his being, and to feel his encompassing love. Through the process of prayer we may grow in love of God and of other people and become less subject to our passions. We may well find that our rhythm prayer reverberates more frequently within us, that the mutual exchange becomes richer and more real, and that prayer plays a more important part in our life. But all this happens very slowly. The process is God's process—what happens within us is governed and controlled not by our own decisions and actions but by God—and God works both secretly and slowly.

This can be frustrating. We would like to make progress as we understand it—to overcome our faults, to become more loving and less selfish, to see ourselves changed—but often this does not seem to happen. We need to accept the slow pace of God's process and to recognize that what God is doing within us is not necessarily what we would like him to do. We discover that many of our imperfections stay with us—and indeed we may discover more imperfections—and we have to learn to live with them. We are not automatically given peace from our passions, and we have to continue to struggle with them. Of course we will hope and long to be better people; but it may be more important in God's eyes that we learn the humility of accepting our imperfections than that we have our imperfections removed. "Those who seek this living union [with God]," says Theophan, "should...not be troubled at their lack of achievement."[4] And Isaac of Nineveh commends "the one who gladly accepts the evil things which cling to him."[5] The most important thing is not to concern ourselves with our own progress in the spiritual life, but to trust that it is indeed God's process and that if we entrust and open ourselves to him he will bring it to the conclusion he chooses. From us God requires patience and waiting.

And what will be the end of the process? Clearly, we do not know precisely. What we will be is a mystery, a secret kept by God. Human eyes have not seen nor ears heard what God has prepared for us. But we can believe that this process leads in the direction of what the early Fathers and many other spiritual writers have called "purity of heart." A pure heart is one that is unencumbered, single in its intention, focused only on God—a heart that is not cluttered up with all kinds of diversions and other pursuits, or clouded by selfish concerns, or covered over by passions; a heart that is clear and luminous like a mirror that seeks God only, loving him above all things. According to the Bible, it is those who have pure hearts who will be able to approach the holy place of God (Ps 24:4) and to "see God" (Matt 5:8). Purity of heart is something we cannot fully attain in this life. It is a quality of heaven. "In the heavenly palace," says Pseudo-Macarius, "those who serve the heavenly King are those who are...pure of heart."[6] But during the course of this life we can grow in purity of heart. As we continue in the life of prayer, we can be moved onward by God's Spirit working within us toward a state in which our hearts are pure, single, and clear, and we are able to "see God."

In the prayer of silence we open ourselves to this mysterious process. To engage deeply in prayer is to embark on the road to purity of heart, and perhaps to be given a taste of it. As we have seen, the deepest prayer, in which the movement of our thoughts ceases and we are totally still before God, is sometimes referred to as "pure prayer." Purity of heart and pure prayer go together. Purity of heart makes for greater purity of prayer; and purity of prayer brings greater purity of heart. "Purity consists of praying to God," says Abba Isaiah;[7] and Aphrahat adds, "Purity of heart constitutes prayer more than do all the prayers that are uttered out aloud."[8] Insofar as we are able in our prayer to descend from our crowded mind into our inner silence and to focus on God alone, we already have a foretaste of this purity, which will be given us in fuller measure later on.

The prayer of silence is, therefore, only a stage on the journey. Prayer itself is an interim activity. It is the mode of our relationship with God during the time of this present life in which we do not have the full, unmediated presence of

God. If we had a direct and immediate relationship with him, prayer would no longer be necessary. "In the life of the spirit," says Isaac of Nineveh, "there is no longer any prayer…. Then both our senses and their operations are superfluous once the soul has become like unto the Godhead by an incomprehensible union."[9] It is true that there are people of profound silent prayer who even in this life have occasionally found themselves taken into a state where they are beyond prayer, where contact with God is so intimate that there is no more place even for "pure prayer"; but this is not normally experienced in this life. We have to await it in the life to come. To enter it we have to undergo a transformation. In the words of Pseudo-Macarius, "Our souls must be changed and transformed from the present state to a new one, to a divine nature."[10] This does not mean that, when this happens, our individual and personal nature will be lost, swallowed up in the mystery of the Godhead, but that there will be a new relationship of oneness in which all that separates us from God will be removed. In the meantime, by patiently continuing the mutual exchange of the prayer of silence, we can cooperate in a process by which, through the gradual purifying of our hearts, we are led toward this state of oneness. When we reach it, the wonderful exchange in which we share through silent prayer will blossom out into a yet more wonderful relationship of immediacy and intimacy with God, which is the final goal of life.

We have to labor and labor, to wait and wait, until the natural is replaced by the grace-given.

(Theophan)[11]

Family life and citizenship are blessed by God, so there is no need to renounce or despise them.

(Theophan)[12]

In the spiritual life there is no place for leaps; what is required is patience.... Prayer requires a struggle until the very hour of death.

(Father John)[13]

This work is not done in one or two days; it needs many years and a long time.

(The Monks Callistus and Ignatius)[14]

This is the great work of a man: always to take the blame for his own sins before God, and to expect temptation to his last breath.

(Anthony the Great)[15]

Oh! the limpid eye which owing to its purity sees unveiled the One at the sight of whom the Seraphim cover their face!...Where then shall God be loved, if not in the heart? and where does he show himself, if not there? Blessed are the pure in heart: they shall see God.

(Sahdona)[16]

Notes

1. Silence: A Mysterious Reality

1. S. Brock, *The Syriac Fathers on Prayer and the Spiritual Life* (Kalamazoo, Mich.: Cistercian Publications, 1987), p. 193.

2. Quoted in H. Alfeyev, *The Spiritual World of Isaac the Syrian* (Kalamazoo, Mich.: Cistercian Publications, 2000), p. 78.

3. Alfeyev, *Isaac the Syrian*, p. 78.

4. Brock, *Syriac Fathers on Prayer*, p. 184.

5. Ibid., p. 349.

6. John Climacus, *The Ladder of Divine Ascent*, trans. C. Luibheid and N. Russell, Classics of Western Spirituality (Mahwah, N.J.: Paulist Press, 1982), p. 159.

7. *Early Fathers from the Philokalia*, trans. E. Kadloubovsky and G. E. H. Palmer (London: Faber & Faber, 1954), p. 140.

8. *The Art of Prayer: An Orthodox Anthology*, ed. Chariton of Valamo (London: Faber & Faber, 1966), p. 147.

9. Olivier Clément, *The Roots of Christian Mysticism* (London: New City, 1993), p. 160.

2. Finding a Way: Some Practical Steps

1. Conference 9:8, in *Western Asceticism,* ed. Owen Chadwick, Library of Christian Classics (Philadelphia: Westminster Press, 1958), p. 218.

2. Father John, *Christ Is in Our Midst: Letters from a Russian Monk* (Crestwood, N.Y.: St. Vladimir's Seminary Press, 1996), pp. 1, 9.

3. Quoted in H. Alfeyev, *The Spiritual World of Isaac the Syrian* (Kalamazoo, Mich.: Cistercian Publications, 2000), p. 184.

4. *Early Fathers from the Philokalia,* trans. E. Kadloubovsky and G. E. H. Palmer (London: Faber & Faber, 1954), p. 206.

5. Ibid., p. 88.

6. Ibid., p. 405.

7. Theophan the Recluse, *The Heart of Salvation* (Newbury, Mass.: Praxis Institute Press, n.d.), p. 147.

8. *The Art of Prayer: An Orthodox Anthology,* ed. Chariton of Valamo (London: Faber & Faber, 1966), p. 104.

9. Ibid., pp. 93, 62.

10. Quoted in Olivier Clément, *The Roots of Christian Mysticism* (London: New City, 1993), p. 202.

11. Teresa of Avila, *Way of Perfection* (London: Sheed & Ward, 1946), p. 130.

12. Ibid., p. 132.

13. Pseudo-Macarius, *Fifty Spiritual Homilies and The Great Letter,* trans. and ed. G. A. Maloney, Classics of Western Spirituality (Mahwah, N.J.: Paulist Press, 1992), p. 194.

14. Ibid., p. 133.

15. Ibid., pp. 45f.

16. Elisabeth Behr-Sigel, *The Place of the Heart: An Introduction to Orthodox Spirituality* (Torrance, Calif.: Oakwood Publications, 1992), p. 98.

17. *Writings from the Philokalia on the Prayer of the Heart,* trans. E. Kadloubovsky and G. E. H. Palmer (London: Faber & Faber, 1951), p. 33.

18. Clément, *Roots,* p. 73.

19. *Art of Prayer,* ed. Chariton, p. 113.

20. John Climacus, *The Ladder of Divine Ascent,* trans. C. Luibheid and N. Russell, Classics of Western Spirituality (Mahwah, N.J.: Paulist Press, 1982), p. 112.

3. Entering Oneself: A Secret Place

1. *Writings from the Philokalia on the Prayer of the Heart,* trans. E. Kadloubovsky and G. E. H. Palmer (London: Faber & Faber, 1951), p. 220.

2. Theophan the Recluse, *The Heart of Salvation* (Newbury, Mass.: Praxis Institute Press, n.d.), p. 103.

3. *The Art of Prayer: An Orthodox Anthology,* ed. Chariton of Valamo (London: Faber & Faber, 1966), p. 184.

4. John Climacus, *The Ladder of Divine Ascent,* trans. C. Luibheid and N. Russell, Classics of Western Spirituality (Mahwah, N.J.: Paulist Press, 1982), p. 75.

5. *Art of Prayer,* ed. Chariton, pp. 67, 60.

6. *Early Fathers from the Philokalia,* trans. E. Kadloubovsky and G. E. H. Palmer (London: Faber & Faber, 1954), p. 132.

7. Olivier Clément, *The Roots of Christian Mysticism* (London: New City, 1993), p. 255.

8. *Art of Prayer,* ed. Chariton, p. 222.

9. Father John, *Christ Is in Our Midst: Letters from a Russian Monk* (Crestwood, N.Y.: St. Vladimir's Seminary Press, 1996), p. 5.

10. Clément, *Roots,* p. 156.

11. *Art of Prayer,* ed. Chariton, pp. 254, 256.

12. Clément, *Roots,* p. 199.

13. Dumitru Staniloae, *Orthodox Spirituality* (South Canaan, Pa.: St. Tikhon's Seminary Press, 2002), p. 286.

14. John Climacus, *Ladder,* p. 238.

15. *Early Fathers from the Philokalia,* p. 301.

16. See Evagrius Ponticus, *The Praktikos and Chapters on Prayer* (Kalamazoo, Mich.: Cistercian Publications, 1972), pp. 16–17.

17. *Early Fathers from the Philokalia,* p. 318.

18. Quoted in Clément, *Roots,* p. 135.

19. Clément, Roots, p. 167.

20. John Climacus, *Ladder,* p. 182.

21. Pseudo-Macarius, *Fifty Spiritual Homilies and The Great Letter,* trans. and ed. G. A. Maloney, Classics of Western Spirituality (Mahwah, N.J.: Paulist Press, 1992), p. 127.

22. *Writings from the Philokalia on the Prayer of the Heart,* p. 23.

23. Archimandrite Hierotheos Vlachos, *A Night in the Desert of the Holy Mountain: Discussion with a Hermit on the Jesus Prayer* (Levadia, Greece: Birth of the Theotokos Monastery, 1991), p. 57.

24. Anthony the Great, *The Letters of Saint Anthony the Great,* trans. Derwas J. Chitty (Oxford: SLG Press, 1975), p. 11.

25. S. Brock, *The Syriac Fathers on Prayer and the Spiritual Life* (Kalamazoo, Mich.: Cistercian Publications, 1992), p. 236–37.

26. Ibid., p. 34.

27. *Art of Prayer,* ed. Chariton, p. 254.

28. Staniloae, *Orthodox Spirituality,* pp. 79, 83.

29. *Early Fathers from the Philokalia,* p. 309.

4. *Encountering God: Shared Subjectivity*

1. *The Art of Prayer: An Orthodox Anthology,* ed. Chariton of Valamo (London: Faber & Faber, 1966), p. 187.

2. Olivier Clément, *The Roots of Christian Mysticism* (London: New City, 1993), p. 231.

3. Dumitru Staniloae, *Orthodox Spirituality* (South Canaan, Pa.: St. Tikhon's Seminary Press, 2002), p. 255.

4. Dumitru Staniloae, *Prayer and Holiness* (Oxford: SLG Press, 1982), pp. 9–10.

5. Pseudo-Macarius, *Fifty Spiritual Homilies and The Great Letter,* trans. and ed. G. A. Maloney, Classics of Western Spirituality (Mahwah, N.J.: Paulist Press, 1992), p. 101.

6. *Art of Prayer,* ed. Chariton, p. 123.

7. Theophan the Recluse, *The Heart of Salvation* (Newbury, Mass.: Praxis Institute Press, n.d.), p. 149.

8. Quoted in S. Brock, *The Luminous Eye: The Spiritual World Vision of Ephrem the Syrian* (Kalamazoo, Mich.: Cistercian Publications, 1992), p. 79.

9. *A Treasury of Russian Spirituality,* ed. G. P. Fedotov (London: Sheed & Ward, 1950), p. 415.

10. Christos Yannaras, *Elements of Faith: An Introduction to Orthodox Theology* (Edinburgh: T. & T. Clark, 1991), p. 29.

11. Archimandrite Sophrony, *The Monk of Mount Athos: Staretz Silouan 1866–1938* (Crestwood, N.Y.: St. Vladimir's Seminary Press, 1973), p. 80.

12. Yannaras, *Elements of Faith*, p. 58.

13. Pseudo-Macarius, *Fifty Spiritual Homilies*, p. 243.

14. *The Sayings of the Desert Fathers: The Alphabetic Collection*, trans. Sr. Benedicta Ward (London: Mowbray, 1975), p. 131.

15. Isaac of Nineveh, *On the Ascetical Life* (Crestwood, N.Y.: St. Vladimir's Seminary Press, 1989), p. 33.

16. *Early Fathers from the Philokalia*, trans. E. Kadloubovsky and G. E. H. Palmer (London: Faber & Faber, 1954), p. 45.

17. Pseudo-Macarius, *Fifty Spiritual Homilies*, p. 194.

18. Quoted in Tomas Spidlík, *The Spirituality of the Christian East: A Systematic Handbook*, trans. Anthony P. Gythiel (Kalamazoo, Mich.: Cistercian Publications, 1986), p. 105.

19. Isaac of Nineveh, *On the Ascetical Life*, p. 73.

20. S. Brock, *The Syriac Fathers on Prayer and the Spiritual Life* (Kalamazoo, Mich.: Cistercian Publications, 1992), pp. 204–5.

21. Staniloae, *Orthodox Spirituality*, p. 289.

22. Vladimir Lossky, *The Mystical Theology of the Eastern Church* (Cambridge: James Clarke, 1957), p. 124.

23. John Climacus, *The Ladder of Divine Ascent*, trans. C. Luibheid and N. Russell, Classics of Western Spirituality (Mahwah, N.J.: Paulist Press, 1982), p. 76.

24. Abba Isaiah, *Ascetic Discourses* (Kalamazoo, Mich.: Cistercian Publications, 2002), p. 60.

25. Ammonas, *The Letters of Ammonas*, trans. Derwas J. Chitty (Oxford: SLG Press, 1979), pp. 11–12.

26. *Early Fathers from the Philokalia*, p. 249.

5. *Mutual Relationship: A Wonderful Exchange*

1. Evagrius Ponticus, *The Praktikos and Chapters on Prayer* (Kalamazoo, Mich.: Cistercian Publications, 1972), p. 64.

2. Pseudo-Macarius, *Fifty Spiritual Homilies and The Great Letter,* trans. and ed. G. A. Maloney, Classics of Western Spirituality (Mahwah, N.J.: Paulist Press, 1992), p. 104.

3. Dumitru Staniloae, *Orthodox Spirituality* (South Canaan, Pa.: St. Tikhon's Seminary Press, 2002), p. 291.

4. *The Art of Prayer: An Orthodox Anthology,* ed. Chariton of Valamo (London: Faber & Faber, 1966), p. 126.

5. Pseudo-Macarius, *Fifty Spiritual Homilies,* p. 201.

6. Quoted in Olivier Clément, *The Roots of Christian Mysticism* (London: New City, 1993), p. 89, and elsewhere.

7. Quoted in Clément, *Roots,* p. 266.

8. John Climacus, *The Ladder of Divine Ascent,* trans. C. Luibheid and N. Russell, Classics of Western Spirituality (Mahwah, N.J.: Paulist Press, 1982), p. 281.

9. *Early Fathers from the Philokalia,* trans. E. Kadloubovsky and G. E. H. Palmer (London: Faber & Faber, 1954), p. 268.

10. Clément, *Roots,* p. 204.

11. Ibid., p. 24.

12. Symeon the New Theologian, *The Discourses,* Classics of Western Spirituality (Mahwah, N.J.: Paulist Press, 1980), p. 142.

13. Pseudo-Macarius, *Fifty Spiritual Homilies,* p. 195.

14. Quoted in Clément, *Roots,* p. 76.

15. Staniloae, *Orthodox Spirituality,* p. 362.

16. Vladimir Lossky, *The Mystical Theology of the Eastern Church* (Cambridge: James Clarke, 1957), p. 155.

6. *Prayer and the World: A Partnership*

1. An explanation given by the translators or editor of *The Art of Prayer: An Orthodox Anthology*, ed. Chariton of Valamo (London: Faber & Faber, 1966), p. 40n.

2. Ibid., p. 147.

3. *Early Fathers from the Philokalia*, trans. E. Kadloubovsky and G. E. H. Palmer (London: Faber & Faber, 1954), p. 76.

4. Archimandrite Sophrony, *The Monk of Mount Athos: Staretz Silouan 1866–1938* (Crestwood, N.Y.: St. Vladimir's Seminary Press, 1973), p. 116.

5. *The Sayings of the Desert Fathers: The Alphabetic Collection*, trans. Sr. Benedicta Ward (London: Mowbray, 1975), p. 134.

6. Sophrony, *Monk of Mount Athos*, p. 86.

7. Quoted in H. Alfeyev, *The Spiritual World of Isaac the Syrian* (Kalamazoo, Mich.: Cistercian Publications, 2000), p. 76.

8. *Sayings of the Desert Fathers*, p. 175.

9. John Climacus, *The Ladder of Divine Ascent*, trans. C. Luibheid and N. Russell, Classics of Western Spirituality (Mahwah, N.J.: Paulist Press, 1982), p. 157.

7. *Prayer and Life: A Process*

1. *The Art of Prayer: An Orthodox Anthology*, ed. Chariton of Valamo (London: Faber & Faber, 1966), p. 134.

2. Theophan the Recluse, *The Heart of Salvation* (Newbury, Mass.: Praxis Institute Press, n.d.), p. 62.

3. Olivier Clément, *The Roots of Christian Mysticism* (London: New City, 1993), p. 146.

4. *Art of Prayer*, ed. Chariton, p. 193.

5. Isaac of Nineveh, *On the Ascetical Life* (Crestwood, N.Y.: St. Vladimir's Seminary Press, 1989), p. 35.

6. Pseudo-Macarius, *Fifty Spiritual Homilies and The Great Letter,* trans. and ed. G. A. Maloney, Classics of Western Spirituality (Mahwah, N.J.: Paulist Press, 1992), p. 125.

7. Abba Isaiah, *Ascetic Discourses* (Kalamazoo, Mich.: Cistercian Publications, 2002), p. 170.

8. S. Brock, *The Syriac Fathers on Prayer and the Spiritual Life* (Kalamazoo, Mich.: Cistercian Publications, 1992), p. 5.

9. Quoted in H. Alfeyev, *The Spiritual World of Isaac the Syrian* (Kalamazoo, Mich.: Cistercian Publications, 2000), pp. 218, 220.

10. Pseudo-Macarius, *Fifty Spiritual Homilies,* p. 225.

11. *Art of Prayer,* ed. Chariton, p. 136.

12. Theophan the Recluse, *Heart of Salvation,* p. 62.

13. Father John, *Christ Is in Our Midst: Letters from a Russian Monk* (Crestwood, N.Y.: St. Vladimir's Seminary Press, 1996), pp. 2, 14.

14. *Writings from the Philokalia on the Prayer of the Heart,* trans. E. Kadloubovsky and G. E. H. Palmer (London: Faber & Faber, 1951), p. 223.

15. *The Sayings of the Desert Fathers: The Alphabetic Collection,* trans. Sr. Benedicta Ward (London: Mowbray, 1975), p. 2.

16. Quoted in Tomas Spidlík, *The Spirituality of the Christian East: A Systematic Handbook,* trans. Anthony P. Gythiel (Kalamazoo, Mich.: Cistercian Publications, 1986), p. 106.

Sources of Quotations

Alfeyev, H. *The Spiritual World of Isaac the Syrian.* Kalamazoo, Mich.: Cistercian Publications, 2000.

Ammonas. *The Letters of Ammonas.* Translated by Derwas J. Chitty. Oxford: SLG Press, 1979.

Anthony the Great. *The Letters of Anthony the Great.* Translated by Derwas J. Chitty. Oxford: SLG Press, 1975.

Behr-Sigel, Elisabeth. *The Place of the Heart: An Introduction to Orthodox Spirituality.* Torrance, Calif.: Oakwood Publications, 1992.

Brock, S. *The Luminous Eye: The Spiritual World Vision of Ephrem the Syrian.* Kalamazoo, Mich.: Cistercian Publications, 1992.

———. *The Syriac Fathers on Prayer and the Spiritual Life.* Kalamazoo, Mich.: Cistercian Publications, 1987.

Chadwick, Owen, ed. *Western Asceticism.* Library of Christian Classics. Philadelphia: Westminster Press, 1958.

Chariton of Valamo, ed. *The Art of Prayer: An Orthodox Anthology.* London: Faber & Faber, 1966.

Clément, Olivier. *The Roots of Christian Mysticism.* London: New City, 1993.

Early Fathers from the Philokalia. Translated by E. Kadloubovsky and G. E. H. Palmer. London: Faber & Faber, 1954.

Evagrius Ponticus. *The Praktikos and Chapters on Prayer*. Translated by John E. Bamberger. Kalamazoo, Mich.: Cistercian Publications, 1972.

Fedetov, G. P., ed. *A Treasury of Russian Spirituality*. London: Sheed & Ward, 1950.

Isaac of Nineveh. *On the Ascetical Life*. Translated by Mary Hansbury. Crestwood, N.Y.: St. Vladimir's Seminary Press, 1989.

Isaiah, Abba. *Ascetic Discourses*. Translated by John Chryssavgis and Pachomios (Robert) Penkett. Kalamazoo, Mich.: Cistercian Publications, 2002.

John, Father. *Christ Is in Our Midst: Letters from a Russian Monk*. Crestwood, N.Y.: St. Vladimir's Seminary Press, 1996.

John Climacus. *The Ladder of Divine Ascent*. Translated by C. Luibheid and N. Russell. Classics of Western Spirituality. Mahwah, N.J.: Paulist Press, 1982.

Lossky, Vladimir. *The Mystical Theology of the Eastern Church*. Cambridge: James Clarke, 1957.

Pseudo-Macarius. *Fifty Spiritual Homilies and The Great Letter*. Translated and edited by G. A. Maloney. Classics of Western Spirituality. Mahwah, N.J.: Paulist Press, 1992.

The Sayings of the Desert Fathers: The Alphabetic Collection. Translated by Sr. Benedicta Ward. London: Mowbray, 1975.

Sophrony, Archimandrite. *The Monk of Mount Athos: Staretz Silouan 1866–1938*. Crestwood, N.Y.: St. Vladimir's Seminary Press, 1973.

Staniloae, Dumitru. *Orthodox Spirituality.* South Canaan, Pa.: St. Tikhon's Seminary Press, 2002.

———. *Prayer and Holiness.* Oxford: SLG Press, 1982.

Symeon the New Theologian. *The Discourses.* Translated by C. J. de Catanzaro. Classics of Western Spirituality. Mahwah, N.J.: Paulist Press, 1980.

Teresa of Avila. *Way of Perfection.* Translated by E. Allison Peers. London: Sheed & Ward, 1946.

Theophan the Recluse. *The Heart of Salvation.* Translated by Esther Williams. Newbury, Mass.: Praxis Institute Press, n.d.

Vlachos, Archimandrite Hierotheos. *A Night in the Desert of the Holy Mountain: Discussion with a Hermit on the Jesus Prayer.* Levadia, Greece: Birth of the Theotokos Monastery, 1991.

Writings from the Philokalia on the Prayer of the Heart. Translated by E. Kadloubovsky and G. E. H. Palmer. London: Faber & Faber, 1951.

Yannaras, Christos. *Elements of Faith: An Introduction to Orthodox Theology.* Edinburgh: T. & T. Clark, 1991.

Appendix:
Notes on Writers
Quoted in the Text

For some of these notes, I have drawn on biographical material in Brock, *The Syriac Fathers on Prayer and the Spiritual Life*; Chariton, ed., *The Art of Prayer*; Clément, *The Roots of Christian Mysticism*; *Early Fathers from the Philokalia*; and *Writings from the Philokalia on the Prayer of the Heart*.

ABBA AMMONAS, ABBA MACARIUS, and ABBA POEMEN were three of the Desert Fathers who lived in the Egyptian desert around the fourth century. Some of their sayings are found in the Alphabetic Collection published as *The Sayings of the Desert Fathers*. There are also a number of letters of Ammonas.

ABRAHAM OF NATHPAR was a monk of the Syrian church associated with Nathpar, near Mosul in modern Iraq. He lived around the turn of the sixth to seventh century. He was the author of a number of texts on the monastic life.

ANTHONY THE GREAT, born in A.D. 251, was the most famous and one of the earliest of the Desert Fathers of Egypt. He spent many years in complete solitude, but was much sought after as a spiritual father. He is the subject of a famous biography by Athanasius, and some of his letters survive.

APHRAHAT lived in the fourth century and is the earliest major Syriac writer whose works survive. He seems to have been a prominent figure in the church in the Persian Empire. He has left twenty-three homilies, many of them dealing with the spiritual life.

BASIL THE GREAT (fourth century) was one of the three famous Cappadocian Fathers of Asia Minor. Having traveled widely and having spent some time in solitude, he later became bishop of Caesarea. He is well known for organizing social work, for establishing monastic communities, and for a number of theological and spiritual writings.

ELISABETH BEHR-SIGEL is a contemporary theologian of the Orthodox Church, based at St. Sergius Orthodox Theological Institute in Paris. She has taught courses and written books and articles on Orthodox spirituality, notably a historical introduction entitled *The Place of the Heart.*

CALLISTUS (fourteenth century), a monk of Mount Athos who became patriarch of Constantinople, and his fellow worker the monk Ignatius, wrote "Directions to Hesychasts," in which they gathered up some of the spiritual teachings of the early Fathers. These are included in the *Philokalia.*

JOHN CASSIAN (fourth to fifth century) provided an important link between the church of the East and that of West. After spending many years among the monks in Egypt, he settled in Marseilles, where he founded monasteries. His *Conferences* on the spiritual life and his *Institutes* on the life of monastic communities are based on his contacts with monks of the desert.

OLIVIER CLÉMENT is a contemporary theologian of the Orthodox Church, based at the St. Sergius Orthodox Theological Institute in Paris. He is the author of many books in different languages, notably *The Roots of Christian Mysticism,* which is frequently quoted in this book.

JOHN CLIMACUS, or John of the Ladder, was a monk and later abbot of the Monastery of St. Catherine at Mount Sinai, in the seventh century. His *Ladder of Divine Ascent,* made up of thirty short treatises or "steps," was based on his own experience as a monk and a solitary. It has had a very great influence on the spiritual life, especially of monks, in the Orthodox Church.

DIMITRI OF ROSTOV was a priest and famous preacher of the Russian Orthodox Church in the seventeenth century, who published a collection of Lives of the Saints. A short work, "The Inner Closet of the Heart," is included in the anthology *The Art of Prayer.*

EPHREM (fourth century), a well-known Syriac writer and poet, served the church in Nisibis and Edessa (in the southeastern part of modern Turkey). He wrote biblical commentaries, meditations, verse homilies, and hymns, and is famous for having expressed profound theology through the medium of poetry.

EVAGRIUS PONTICUS was a very famous and controversial Greek writer of the fourth century, originally from Pontus in Asia Minor. Having been prominent in the church in Constantinople and Jerusalem, he finally moved to Egypt and spent his last years in the desert. His *Praktikos,* on the spiritual life, and his *Chapters on Prayer,* had a great influence on the theory and practice of contemplative prayer.

GREGORY PALAMAS was a monk of Mount Athos and archbishop of Thessalonica in the fourteenth century. He was a leader and exponent of the doctrine and spiritual path known as "hesychasm," or "way of silence." He developed the use of the Jesus Prayer as a way of reaching toward undisrupted communion with God and a vision of his glory.

IGNATII BRIANCHANINOV was a monk and bishop of the Russian Orthodox Church in the nineteenth century, who retired into solitude and devoted his energies to writing and spiritual direction. Some of his writings are included in *The Art of Prayer.*

ISAAC OF NINEVEH (seventh century) was one of the most profound writers of the Syriac churches. Born in Qatar, he became bishop of Nineveh (modern Mosul), but later retired into solitude. He wrote a number of spiritual discourses that have had an enormous influence on the spirituality of the Christian East.

ABBA ISAIAH was a monk of the fifth century who was well known in Egypt until he moved to Palestine in search of greater solitude. Later, through a disciple, he supervised a monastery at Gaza and wrote a series of *Discourses* to provide training and instruction in monastic living.

JOHN, known as Father John, was head of the monastery of the Russian Orthodox Church at Valamo in Finland in the early years of the twentieth century. He wrote many letters of spiritual counsel, some of which are published under the title *Christ Is in Our Midst.*

JOHN OF CRONSTADT, or John Sergieff, was a parish priest of the Orthodox Church in Russia in the nineteenth century. His spiritual diary, published under the title *My Life in Christ,* gives practical and personal advice especially on prayer.

VLADIMIR LOSSKY, a distinguished twentieth-century theologian of the Russian Orthodox Church in France, is the author of *The Mystical Theology of the Eastern Church,* an influential exposition of Orthodox theology.

PSEUDO-MACARIUS is the name given to an unknown Syrian monk, probably of the fourth century, who left a large number of spiritual homilies that emphasize the heart as the place of prayer and the inner experience of union with Christ. His writings have been influential both in the East and in the West.

MARK THE ASCETIC was a hermit of the Egyptian desert in the fourth to fifth centuries who is believed to have written a number of works. Not many of his writings survive, but some are included in the *Philokalia.*

MAXIMUS THE CONFESSOR was an important theologian of the seventh century, born in Constantinople, who traveled widely and was engaged in the controversies of his time. His extensive and influential spiritual writings, written mostly in Carthage, include analysis of the passions and an emphasis on *kenōsis* or self-emptying.

NICEPHORUS, known as "the Solitary," was a monk of Mount Athos in the early fourteenth century. His writings, some of which are in the *Philokalia,* include discussion of the practice of inner prayer and excerpts from the works of earlier Fathers. He is important for his influence on Gregory Palamas.

NILUS (fourth to fifth century) left an important government position in Antioch to live an austere life in the desert of Mount Sinai. A number of texts on prayer are in his name in the *Philokalia,* but some of them were originally from the hand of Evagrius and were wrongly attributed to Nilus.

SAHDONA, also known as Martyrius, was a monk and bishop in what is now northern Iraq, in the seventh century. His writings include *The Book of Perfection,* one of the master-pieces of Syriac monastic literature, in which he emphasizes the interior offering of the heart and the importance of reverence in the presence of God.

SILOUAN was a monk of the Russian monastery on Mount Athos in the nineteenth to twentieth century known for his simplicity, humility, and spiritual wisdom. His life and sayings are recorded in two small books by his disciple Archimandrite Sophrony.

DUMITRU STANILOAE was a priest and distinguished theologian of the Orthodox Church in Romania in the twentieth century. His many works, including a pamphlet published by the SLG Press and a major work entitled *Orthodox Spirituality,* reflect both the hesychast tradition and the spiritual tradition of Romania.

SYMEON THE NEW THEOLOGIAN (tenth to eleventh century) was an abbot in Constantinople, later exiled to a town across the Bosphorus. His *Discourses,* or addresses to his monks, in which he emphasized the direct experience of God in the heart of the individual, became very famous and influential in the Orthodox Church.

THEOPHAN THE RECLUSE (nineteenth century) was a theologian of the Russian Church in St. Petersburg, and later a bishop, who spent the last twenty-eight years of his life in solitude and prayer. He conducted a vast correspondence on spiritual matters with people from all over Russia, placing special emphasis on "the mind in the heart" in prayer. Some of his writings form the larger part of the volume on *The Art of Prayer.*

ARCHIMANDRITE HIEROTHEOS VLACHOS is a contemporary priest of the Greek Orthodox Church and author of popular Greek books on spirituality. The book quoted here records discussions with a hermit on Mount Athos on the Jesus Prayer and the prayer of the heart.

CHRISTOS YANNARAS is a contemporary theologian of the Greek Orthodox Church and a professor in Athens. He is the author of a number of books on theology and philosophy. His *Elements of Faith* aims to introduce the Western mind to some of the distinctive features of the Orthodox tradition.